HAWICK

A History from Earliest Times

Alistair Moffat

First published in 2014 by
Birlinn Limited
West Newington House
10 Newington Road
Edinburgh
EH9 1QS

www.birlinn.co.uk

ISBN: 978 1 78027 229 0

British Library Cataloguing-in-Publication Data
A catalogue record for this book is available from the British Library

Typeset by Iolaire Typesetting, Newtonmore
Printed and bound by Gutenberg Press, Malta

For Ellen Irvine

CONTENTS

List of Illustrations ix
Introduction – The Irvines xi

1 Hornshole 1
2 Hawick among the Hills 9
3 Aye Defend 41
4 The Coming of the Wolves 65
5 The Lords of the Names 89
6 Cornets, the Common and Carterhaugh 109
7 Hardie's Hawick 121
8 Hawick Lost and Found 149

Index 185

LIST OF ILLUSTRATIONS

The Mote, photographed in 1912

Auld Mid Raw, demolished in1884

Hawick Common Riding, 1902, led by Cornet William N. Graham

Hawick Railway Station, 1903

A cavalry regiment at Stobs Camp, 1904

Stobs Camp Post Office and a group of regimental postmen, 1905

The unveiling of The Horse by Lady Sybil Scott in June 1914

The 400th anniversary celebrations of Hornshole in 1914 at the Volunteer Park

The Chase

An autographed portrait of the great Jimmy Guthrie

Manly support – made in Hawick

Jimmy Guthrie's characteristic riding style

Jack Anderson, Hawick and Scotland, Huddersfield and Great Britain

Hawick RFC, Border and Scottish Champions, 1959–60

Bill McLaren

INTRODUCTION

THE IRVINES

'AYE DEFEND!'

Startled, I looked up at my mum in terrified astonishment.

'Aye defend your rights and Common!' she shouted as the Cornet raised up the banner and the High Street crowd roared its support.

My mum never shouted at home in Kelso – not even when she had cause, usually supplied by me. A gigantic, snorting horse suddenly clattered sideways and I skittered behind her. But she cheered all the more and muffled, from somewhere, I could hear, 'Hip, hip, hooray! Hip, hip, hooray! Hip, hip, hooray!' The riders and the flag moved on, the crowd followed and I stopped clutching my mum's hand so tightly.

When she came home to Hawick for the Common Riding, my mum became a different person. Although I did not understand it at the time, she came home every summer to be herself again – a Teri (a native of Hawick), a sister, a cousin, a niece, a girlhood friend and not just a mother. Born Ellen Irvine at Allars Crescent when it was a bowed row of tenements behind the west end of the High Street, she had seen Cornets raise the banner high only yards away from where she had grown up. The summer colour of the rideouts, the songs, the chase, the Mair and the shows at the Haugh were bright threads woven into her earliest days. One of seven sisters and a solitary brother, my mum was raised in a tiny flat, in the body warmth of a crowded, noisy and vivid family. Seventy years later, when my dad died, her bewilderment was more than emotional. She told me it would be the first time in her life she had not shared a bed.

At the Common Ridings, I inherited a powerful sense of the closeness of the Irvines. My aunties Mary, Jean, Daisy, Isa and Margaret and my uncle David all gathered at the Mair, always spreading out rugs and a vast picnic at what seemed to be exactly the same place. Even the ghost of Auntie Mina, who died before we could know her, seemed to linger there. In the June sunshine, we celebrated. With all my Hawick cousins, there must have been thirty or forty eating sandwiches, drinking lemonade or something stronger, watching the races, the purples, yellows, reds, blues and greens of the jockeys' silks shining in the sun, the rumble of hoof beats, the cheering crowds, my aunties shaking their heads at one or two neighbours who had celebrated too well and appeared to have lost control of their legs.

In those distant summers of the 1950s and early 1960s, Hawick seemed to me a wonderland of generous laughter and music. Exotic too – the shows at the Haugh smelled of spun candyfloss, hot dogs and onions, and in the air was the faint, electric whiff of disrepute. I loved it. My uncles often gave me a half-crown so that I could go on the dodgems or the Waltzer or shoot tiny, feathered darts out of ancient rifles with bent barrels. As the men jingled change in the pockets of their flannels – their tweed sports jackets, Van Heusen shirts and club ties immaculate – and the women wore new dresses, it occurred to me that Hawick people had come to their own party. There was a sense of a long celebration punctuated by mysterious rituals everyone understood, gatherings at specific places at specific times and a simple pride. Hawick was all dressed up to celebrate no more and no less than itself.

There was also a palpable sense of escape. From the deafening rattle and clack of the mills where most of my aunties worked, they were released into the June sunshine for the Common Riding. The mills fell silent then but, for the rest of the year, they meant money and, more significantly, money for women, who were in a large majority on the dozens of weaving and knitting flats. Nimble fingers, a keen eye and an uncomplaining attitude to the endless repetition of textile production had delivered jobs in abundance for women. When I began to go to Hawick Common Riding with my mum in the mid 1950s and into the 1960s, there was money in Hawick and most of it in purses and handbags rather than wallets and back pockets.

Although I did no more than intuit it at the time, Hawick women, and especially Irvine women, were vivid, even exuberant. 'Weel pit oan, like maist Hawick folk, and aye plenty to say for theirsells' was my dad's description and, with the help of exclusive access to the mill sales, there was plenty of cashmere and high quality tweed on view at the Mair and the grand occasions of the Common Riding.

Hawick women also had an independent, adventurous streak. My auntie Jean was holidaying in Majorca long before the arrival of the package tourists and she even had a special, posh wee handbag-like thing she kept her fags in. Never afraid to speak her mind, if she could get a word in edgeways with her sisters, Jean also had a stock of risqué stories that came straight out of the mills. Much enhanced by the relative prosperity in the manufacture of knitwear, hosiery and tweed, the status of women in Hawick was high. I remember all my uncles very fondly but they are snapshots in black and white while my aunties lived in vivid Technicolor.

Compared to douce, well-set Kelso, essentially a market town in the 1950s serving the rich farmlands of the lower Tweed Valley, Hawick seemed metropolitan. When we stayed with Auntie Jean at her flat at the top of Gladstone Street, we went out to the pictures – almost every night. Not only was there a rapid turnover of films at the Kings and the Piv (I had to look this up, The Pavilion, long disappeared, was its Sunday name), they were shown on a continuous loop. This amazed me. You only had to pay once and you could watch everything at least twice. More amazing, my mum and my auntie Jean took me and my sisters into a film halfway through – and then we waited for it to start again so that we could see how it began. I can remember blue cigarette smoke curling upwards through the beam of the projector. And then my mum would get to say, 'This is where we came in.' and we would leave. Usually I managed to persuade a detour to the chip shop in Silver Street, if we were at the King's, or a visit to Taddei's Cafe in the High Street. It was famous because my cousin Carl once knocked over a big glass container of peanuts and it smashed on the floor.

Hawick's sense of otherness, of being different from its neighbouring Border towns was of course heightened by language. *Yow*, *mei*, *sei* and *hyim* were immediately recognisable to me as 'you', 'me', 'see' and 'home' because that was how my family spoke. Not strange or difficult, it was the language of warmth, celebration, good jokes, relish and directness. Relish and directness because the Hawick accent encourages full value for every syllable, nothing is glossed over, literally, and its insistence is total. When my cousin Janet announced that she did not much care for me – 'Hei is horreebull!' – no doubt was possible.

Men asserted themselves mightily in one huge aspect of life. Rugby was dominant in the Borders in the 1950s and 1960s. And rugby was the only thing I didn't like about Hawick. They won all the time. And reared, but never sated, on season after season of unremitting success, Hawick rugby crowds could be tribal. If, by some rare refereeing mischance, Hawick were knocked out of a Borders sevens tournament, the terraces thinned dramatically as the Hawick fans simply went home. At the end of the 1960s, I played for Kelso against Hawick in a couple of tournaments and, while the players had the confidence of repeated success (they won both ties), the crowd was nevertheless visceral. When I tackled a Hawick player on the touchline at Riverside Park and momentum carried us skidding to the feet of the packed crowd, a voice hissed, 'Dirty Kelsae bastard.' and another spat at me. Only eighteen, I was taken aback.

Probably wisely, my mum never came to see me play. But she could be quietly fierce about things that really mattered and, looking back now, I can see that her independent strength of will and mind had much to do with her upbringing. My mum deferred to no one, believed that no one had any right to call themselves better. Richer certainly, better educated probably, taller obviously, but never innately better. That belief in a fundamental egalitarianism developed into an equality of regard. Everyone, no matter how humble or exalted their circumstances, had the right to an equality of regard and my mum never wavered from that. In her eyes, dustmen and dukes deserved respect that was theirs to lose.

Much of her sense of herself and other people sprang from her utter decency and enveloping warmth but some of it was also learned as she grew up in Allars Crescent in the 1920s. 'Aye defend your rights and Common!' was shouted with conviction for my mum believed it, believed in the fundamental democracy of a community of ordinary people lining their streets to hail one of their own as he passed with the town standard, the emblem of that democracy, in his working man's hand. Like many of the Border principals, Hawick Cornets are chosen precisely because they are ordinary citizens who have demonstrated a simple love for the place where they were born. And, from that central, irreducible feature, the commonality of the Common Riding flourishes. It is a celebration of Hawick and everyone in it, regardless of status or money. All you have to be is a Teri. And my mum first imbibed that sense of simple democracy as a child and grew into a woman who believed in it absolutely.

Despite all of the reverses, closures and failures of recent years – even the humbling of the great rugby team – the flame of the Common Riding still burns brightly. All that it symbolises still lives and thrives in Hawick. It remains a remarkable, utterly different place and its story is never less than fascinating. My mum, Ellen Irvine, never lost her love for the town and never misplaced its values. I am honoured to be her son and, in inadequate thanks for all the love she gave me, this book is dedicated to her memory.

Alistair Moffat,
January 2014

1

HORNSHOLE

When dawn broke on the morning of 10 September 1513, the landscape of hell was revealed. On the gently undulating northern ridges of Branxton Hill, more than 10,000 men lay dead or dying. In the midst of the carnage were the naked, plundered bodies of King James IV of Scotland, Alexander Stewart, Archbishop of St Andrews, George Hepburn, Bishop of the Isles, two abbots, nine great earls of Scotland, fourteen lords of parliament, innumerable knights and noblemen of lesser degree and thousands of ploughmen, farmers, weavers and burgesses. It was the appalling aftermath of the Battle of Flodden, the greatest military disaster in Scotland's history.

In the grey light of that terrible dawn, sentries posted around the captured Scottish cannon could make out where the brunt of battle had been joined. Below them, at the foot of the slope, ran the trickle of a nameless burn now piled with slaughter, a wrack of bodies, obscenely mangled, broken pike shafts, shattered shields and everywhere blood and the sickening stench of death, vomit and voided bowels. Not all of the bodies were yet corpses. Through a long dark night, the battlefield had not been a silent graveyard. Trapped under lifeless comrades, crippled, hamstrung or horribly mutilated, fatally wounded men still breathed. Bladed weapons rarely kill outright and they were often used to bludgeon men to their knees or into unconsciousness. In the churned mud of the battlefield, some men will have lost their footing, fallen and been hacked at before they could get up. Many bled to death, maimed, lacerated by vicious cuts, screaming, fainting and screaming once more in their death agonies. Some will have been put out of their misery by parties of English soldiers scouring the field by torchlight for plunder but others will have lingered on in unspeakable pain, praying to their god, passing in and out of consciousness. The fury of the battlefield may have been stilled and Flodden Field awash with death and defeat but all was not yet over.

In an instant, the plunderers looked up and the sentries by the cannon stood to, clutching at their weapons, frantically peering through the morning light. They could hear the rumbling thunder of hoof beats – and then suddenly riders erupted over Bareless Rig. With 800 horsemen at his back, Lord Alexander Home galloped hard across the horrors of the battlefield and up the slopes of Branxton Hill. They had not come back to Flodden to rejoin a lost battle but to rescue their captured ordnance. And they very nearly succeeded. After a sharp skirmish, the English gunners managed to load and get off a volley at Home's squadron and they scattered.

And so it ended. And the Border horsemen wheeled round and raced out of range. To the north, having crossed the Tweed by the morning of 10 September, the remnants of the defeated Scottish army limped homewards. There appears to have been no organised pursuit for, although between 5,000 and 8,000 Scots had been killed at Flodden Field, the Earl of Surrey's army had also taken severe casualties. But those Englishmen who fell were, for the most part, ordinary foot soldiers. King James himself led the downhill charge of his own battalion, running towards the enemy, and most of his noblemen did the same. They led from the front and, when the grim scrummage of hand-to-hand fighting went against them, the king, his earls and his knights were amongst the first to be cut down and killed, unable to retreat, trapped in a murderous, fatal vice. By contrast, the Earl of Surrey and his captains had stationed themselves behind their lines and could direct the flow of the battle, making judgements, issuing orders. Submerged in the ruck of the front rank, James IV and his earls were impotent and, having become foot soldiers able to see only what was directly in front of them, they left the huge Scottish army leaderless. It was a critical, determinant distinction between the two sides.

Lord Home and the Earl of Huntly were in command of the battalion on the left wing of the Scottish army and were the first to engage. The Border pikemen and Huntly's Highlanders drove through the English ranks and a rout was only prevented when the Cumbrian baron Lord Dacre ordered his cavalry to charge into the melee. But, when the king's massive battalion of 9,000 men locked with the centre of Surrey's forces and the English billmen began to turn the battle into butchery, Home and Huntly became detached. Able to rally their men on the higher ground to the south-west, they saw that history was moving below them, turning against Scotland. In the rear of the Scottish battalions, the less well-armed, less disciplined and much less motivated ordinary soldiers could see the Scottish pikes falling in front of them and their lords and captains going down with them. Many turned away and fled, following Home and Huntly as they led their men off the field in some order. Many Borderers will have gone with them, saving themselves from the slaughter.

Douglases fell at Flodden. In the front rank, Sir William Douglas of Drumlanrig, Baron of Hawick, was hacked to death by the billmen. It is said that two hundred of his kinsmen were killed by his side. While there exists no firm documentary evidence to corroborate this tradition, a similar fate certainly befell William Hay, the Earl of Erroll, and his retinue. Eighty-seven Hays died with him. Flodden devastated Scotland's noble families and, while many ordinary soldiers were cut down (amongst the battalion of Highlanders led by the Earls of Argyll and Lennox, there was great carnage when they were attacked by English archers), it seems likely that Borderers did not suffer as badly as traditions – and music – insist.

I've heard the lilting, at the yowe-milking,
Lassies a-lilting before dawn o' day;
But now they are moaning on ilka green loaning;
'The Flowers of the Forest are a' wede away.'

Jean Elliot's lyrics of 1756 imply that Flodden saw many Border flowers 'wede away' and the ancient air is played at the Casting of the Colours at Selkirk Common Riding each year when it is understood as a lament and a commemoration of the battle. While many Borderers were undoubtedly killed, the association may well be overstated.

It was Scotland's auld alliance with France that induced James IV to invade England and thereby open up a second front while Henry VIII was campaigning across the Channel. But less than a year after Flodden, England made peace with France and French support for Scotland ceased immediately. Without any consultation or even foreknowledge, the treaty included Scotland by expressly forbidding any raiding into England – but not English raiding into Scotland. By the standards of any age, it was a cynical sell-out – the abandonment of an ally so recently devastated in a battle fought in a common cause.

In the winter months of 1513 and a year later, in 1514, several English raiding parties were reiving cattle and burning farms in Tweeddale and Teviotdale. Aside from the skirmish at Sclaterford on the Rule Water near Bonchester Bridge in November 1513, few reports of incidents have found their way into the historical record but there is no doubt that serial mischief took place in the aftermath of the great slaughter. While the armies clashed at the foot of Branxton Hill, Scottish and English thieves, the forerunners of the Border Reivers, had attacked the English camp at Barmoor, two miles to the east. According to a contemporary chronicler, 'Many men lost their horses, and such stuff as they left in their tents and pavilions, by the robbers of Tynedale and Tweeddale.'

For exhausted soldiers who had survived and won a bloody battle, their return to a plundered camp would have left a bitter and lasting taste. It may be that a year later some would ride back into the Scottish

Border country in search of revenge. But one particular party of English raiders in one particular place would be disappointed.

Under the patronage of Lord Thomas Dacre, the Cumbrian baron whose cavalry had driven off Home and Huntly the year before, a group of raiders had been encouraged to take advantage of the victory at Flodden. In 1514, Dacre sent a despatch to Cardinal Wolsey, Henry VIII's principal minister saying, 'There was never so much mischief, robbery, spoiling and vengeance in Scotland as there is now, without hope of remedy, which I pray our Lord God to continue.' And it did. A party of English horsemen had corralled a pack of stolen beasts at Hornshole, on the banks of the Teviot two miles east of Hawick. The place name probably derives from Heron's Hole, a favoured fishing-place for those elegant birds once memorably described as Presbyterian flamingos. Other possible meanings are Orm's Hole, after the same Anglian lord who gave his name to Ormiston, or Orm's Tun. Less likely is Hornie's Hole, a deep dwelling place for the Devil – although diabolical doings are an understandable association with the times local people were living in. Perhaps the advancing English raiders planned to assault the village and the farms around that stretch of the Teviot. A powerful oral tradition recounts that a party of young men from Hawick mustered and, at night, attacked the enemy encampment. Called 'callants' (an unusual term, cognate to the Latin verb *calere*, 'to warm', and probably carrying the sense 'hotheads'), they are said to have scattered the raiding party and captured their flag.

Where documentary history is silent or lost, the imagination of the great Hawick poet, James Hogg, rushed in to fill the vacuum. Here is his description of events at Hornshole followed by the rousing chorus of 'Teribus':

All were sunk in deep dejection,
None to flee to for protection;
Till some youths who stayed from Flodden,
Rallied up by Teriodin.

Armed with sword with bow and quiver,
Shouting 'Vengeance now or never',
Off they marched in martial order
Down by Teviot's flowery border.

Nigh where Teviot falls sonorous
Into Hornshole dashing furious,
Lay their foes with spoil encumbered;
All was still, each sentry slumbered.

Hawick destroyed, their slaughtered sires –
Scotia's wrongs each bosom fires –
On they rush to be victorious,
Or to fall in battle glorious.

Down they threw their bows and arrows,
Drew their swords like veteran heroes,
Charged their foe with native valour,
Routed them and took their colour.

Now with spoil and honours laden,
Well revenged for native Flodden,
Home they marched, this flag displaying –
Teribus before them playing.

Teribus ye Teri Odin,
Sons of heroes slain at Flodden,
Imitating Border bowmen.
Aye defend your rights and Common.

Much has been made of this incident – indeed, some would argue that the complex traditions of Hawick's Common Riding are built on it. Encouraged by Hogg's skill, there is a widely held belief that the young callants or hotheads were somehow taking revenge for 'the sons of Hawick who fell at Flodden' and that the village and surrounding area had been emptied of older men – those who had died in battle a year before.

Much more likely is that many of the local lairds had been killed – the Douglases of Hawick and Cavers had certainly suffered loss but other notables had as well – and, in military terms, the community lacked leadership. It is important to grasp what this meant. As Baron of Hawick, Sir William Douglas owned the village (it was not yet a town) and much of the land around it. The inhabitants owed him services – almost all of them related to food production of one sort or another. Douglas had absolute power over his tenants and he would not have hesitated to assert it by force. Equally, he and his household would have protected their assets, the village and the neighbouring farmland, by force. But, in 1514, it is very likely that central authority in Hawick, Cavers and elsewhere had been cut to pieces on Flodden field and whoever was left in Drumlanrig's Tower was female, very young or too powerless to take any initiative.

In these unusual circumstances, a much more attractive interpretation of the events that led to Hornshole suggests itself. Instead of cowering, waiting for the attack or fleeing into the hills, the callants acted on their own initiative to protect their people and what property they had. Without the need for aristocratic direction, they acted together in the common interest – aye defend your rights and Common! It was the beginning of a long, proud and immensely impressive tradition of Hawick helping herself.

2

HAWICK AMONG THE HILLS

On the rocky western coast of the Isle of Man near the hamlet of Niarbyl, the cliffs of a secluded cove have preserved something unique – the key to understanding the geology and the landscape of the Borders. A thin, greyish-white seam of rock runs diagonally down to the shore and disappears below the waves. It marks exactly the point at which two gigantic continents collided an unimaginably long time ago and it is the only place on Earth where what is known as the Iapetus Suture can be clearly seen. Between 480 and 430 million years ago, a vast prehistoric sea called the Iapetus Ocean was shrinking. It lay between three palaeocontinents – Laurentia, Baltica and Avalonia. The Earth's crust was still young, forming and reforming vast landmasses. The immensely powerful phenomenon of tectonic shift was moving Laurentia, Baltica and Avalonia ever closer together and the Iapetus Ocean was narrowing. This remote episode of geological drama would determine the shape and nature of Borders landscape and throw up the hills that shelter Hawick.

On the southern edge of Laurentia lay the land that would become Scotland and on the northern shore of Avalonia was much of what would become England and Wales. When the palaeocontinents finally collided, a process lasting many millennia, they squeezed up the Southern Uplands between them, and the angle of the collision laid down the fundamental shape of Borders geography. Broadly, the ranges of hills and the course of rivers and their valleys run south-west to north-east precisely because of the way in which Laurentia and Avalonia were pushed into each other.

Differences in the nature of rock had the second determinant effect. When the much harder rocks of Scotland/Laurentia ground into England/Avalonia, scraping and crumpling together like an extremely slow-motion collision, they buckled and twisted the softer southern formations. The tremendous energy of the tectonic shift pushed up seams of coal and iron ore much nearer to the surface and, many millions of years later, the heavy industries of West Cumbria and Tyneside would be founded on this geological quirk. And, while the Industrial Revolution rumbled into life and mines were sunk into the softer seams to the south, the hard rock of the north would underpin some of the most fertile agricultural areas of Scotland.

Laurentia, Baltica and Avalonia formed part of Pangea, the massive single landmass that existed for millions of years surrounded by a vast ocean. It fragmented but, joined by the Iapetus Suture, Scotland and England stuck together. And geology influenced politics directly and the compass direction of the border between the two nations runs from the north-east to the south-west along the Cheviot watershed because of an ancient collision. That the collision at Flodden happened where it did is an accident of geology as much as history. And, when the hills and valleys of the Borders rose up out of the waters of the Iapetus Ocean more than 400 million years ago, that little known episode of tectonic drama merely served to underpin something that Borderers have always known – that our landscape and people are unique, not a part of Scotland or England but independent of either.

Around 350 million years ago, the tranquil plains of Pangea shuddered and suddenly erupted as a series of events of astonishing violence began. From the mouths of volcanoes, huge tonnages of ash, dust and pumice rocketed into the atmosphere, great storms blew, thunder boomed and rivers of white-hot lava flowed. Cheviot may be the stump of a gigantic volcano and the Eildon Hills the north-western rim of another but surely the most perfect relic of several eras of volcanic violence is the conical shape of Ruberslaw.

All of these hills are but a shadow of what they once were. Aeons of erosion have diminished them and, around a million years ago, the fire and thunder that spewed from their summits was stilled by the first of many ice ages. The most recent ended only 13,000 years ago – a mere blink of the eye in geological time. In places, ice-sheets more than a kilometre thick crushed what would become Scotland and the pitiless white landscape was dominated by vast, spherical ice-domes. One of these formed over Ben Lomond and, around its foot, cycles of low pressure brought near-constant hurricane-force winds, their velocity increased by the smoothness of the ice. Above them, on the summits of the ice-domes, high pressure produced endless days of dazzling sunshine. But it warmed nothing. At the height of the last ice age, around 16,000 BC, no plant, no insect, no animal, no human being could live in what was a desert of devastating beauty. And, under this thick and sterile blanket, Scotland slept, waiting to form, waiting for its green grasses, flowers and trees, its animals and, ultimately, its people.

When the thaw at last came, around 11,000 BC, it was dynamic. As the ice-domes began to splinter and crack and glaciers ground slowly down from their summits, they began to shape Scotland's landscape. Singular and famous features like Stirling and Edinburgh castle rocks show the direction in which the melting ice moved. The tails of land on the eastern sides of both rocks (where people eventually began to build houses) and the sheer cliffs on the west are incontrovertible proof that the glaciers moved eastwards down the slopes of the Lomond ice-dome.

The same effects influenced the Borders landscape profoundly. As the ice scarted and ground its way eastwards, it carried along much debris. Locked into the mighty glaciers were huge boulders, pods of gravel and much else. Like prehistoric sandpaper, they scoured out the river valleys of the Borders, directing them eastwards to the North

Sea. And fertile Berwickshire, eastern Roxburghshire and north Northumberland were where the ingredients that made the best soil on the flatter land were bulldozed and dumped. And, in western Roxburghshire, the ice broke out the watercourses that would become the Slitrig and the Teviot.

Scientists now believe that the ice retreated quickly – perhaps over the course of only a handful of generations. As the land warmed and summers lengthened, a green carpet of vegetation crept northwards. On what had been polar tundra, grass began to grow and, in sheltered places, willow scrub, birch and alder seeded and slowly spread. Watered by spring rains, pasture colonised the Tweed and Teviot valleys and herds of grazing animals followed it northwards. Wild horses, reindeer, elk and bison roamed the open spaces, always alert for predators. Cave lions, lynx and wolf packs circled the herds, searching out old, young or weak stragglers.

Behind the seasonal migrations of the great herds came their most deadly predator – human beings. Soon after the ice finally retreated, pioneers came north and traces of a very early encampment have been found at Cramond, near Edinburgh. It dates between 9,000 BC and 8,500 BC but all that excavators could scrape at carefully with their trowels were the remains of waste pits, soil discolourations where fires had been lit, some hazelnuts shells (organic matter crucial for radiocarbon dating) and stake-holes that once supported shelters.

Much more substantial was a remarkable find near the farm of East Barns. To the east of Dunbar, not far from the A1, archaeologists came across a circle of massive postholes, each large enough to accommodate a trimmed tree trunk. The angle at which the holes had been dug indicated that the trunks had been canted inward to form a conical structure, perhaps lashed together at the top or simply locked in place by its own weight. This was no mere shelter but a substantial and sophisticated house – and it dated to 8,000 BC. The construction implied all sorts of revisions. The pioneers who came north after the ice were hunter-gatherers, people who harvested wild fruits, roots, fungi, nuts (like the hazelnuts at Cramond), hunted animals and fished. Virtually nomadic, they were thought to have flitted through the landscape, barely rustling the leaves, leaving little trace of their passing. But here at East Barns was a house, a huge investment in labour, large enough to sleep eight to ten people – a family band who will have regarded it as their own and also claimed ownership of the land around it.

Coastal sites like Cramond and East Barns were good places to live 10,000 years ago. The landward area provided natural resources such as wood, stone and bracken for roofing and insulation and fresh water as well as its bounty of flora and fauna. In winter, when the land was less productive, the sea could be fished and mussel and oyster beds harvested at low tide. Many of the earliest settlements in northern Britain are to be found near the sea.

Pioneers preferred seaside sites for another simple reason. They knew where they were and could travel quickly and easily between locations – by water. The ancient technology of coracle and curragh construction is still alive in southern Ireland and skilled men can put together a well-made craft from greenwood rods, cord and fabric (instead of expensive hide) in a morning. These boats were undoubtedly widely used in prehistory, although it must be said that their wholly organic and relatively flimsy nature has meant that no sign of them exists in the archaeological record. Two of the many advantages of curraghs (coracles are rounder and generally used on lakes while curraghs are more canoe-shaped) were that they were light and easily carried and that they needed very little depth of water to float.

As men sailed along the coasts of the Firth of Forth after 8,000 BC, their landward vista contrasted sharply with the open sea. It was green and almost impenetrable. Trees had begun to grow and, as the weather warmed, they reached high altitudes, much higher than in modern times. Willow, birch and alder had been first but then came mighty oaks and tall elms. By 6,000 BC, Scotland was covered by the wildwood, a temperate jungle where the only paths were made by animals, where the overhead canopy was dense and at ground level it was humid and very shaded. The prey animals of the grassland plains had been replaced by forest species, some of them very dangerous. Brown bears browsed the undergrowth, fished the streams and no doubt searched for wild honey. The bones of wild boar have been unearthed on the banks of the Tweed near Coldstream and those of the huge wild cattle known as aurochs found at Synton Moss between Hawick and Selkirk. They were herbivorous but almost six-foot tall at the shoulder and, with a lyre-shaped horn spread of more than three feet, viciously pointed, they were not to be disturbed. Less alarming, beavers dammed the streams of the wildwood in the Borders and the remains of a birch wood felled by them around 5,000 BC have been identified near Earlston.

Hawick is about as far from the sea as it is possible to be in Scotland. Nevertheless pioneer bands did penetrate far inland – and very early. Some time around 6,000 BC, men and women cleared part of the wildwood near Teviothead. Pollen cores drilled out of peaty, anaerobic soil revealed data indicating that trees were felled or burned back at that time. Hunters may have been creating clearings where woodland animals could graze and drink and present themselves as easier prey.

These pioneers used rivers as their highways. It was easy to become lost in the dense and dark green of the wildwood and, if they came into the Borders from the east, up the wide mouth of the Tweed, their navigators will have quickly developed a mental map of the river system. Paddling where possible, picking up their curraghs on what they hoped were short portages, noting junctions with tributaries and recognisable geographical features near riverbanks, they will have penetrated far inland, perhaps at first on summer expeditions. Or perhaps the woodland clearers at Teviothead came from the west, by the Esk and the Ewes, before climbing the Mosspaul watershed.

Who were these people? Brave, resourceful and adventurous, they certainly came from the south. As the ice retreated and what became Scotland warmed, all of the first new arrivals came from the south

– but from where exactly? That is not an impossible question to ask about people who lived 8,000 years ago. Borderers carry the answer in their bodies.

Far to the south, during the long millennia when the hurricanes whistled around the foot of the ice-domes over Scotland, human beings were sheltering from the cold and bitter weather. In the deep river valleys of the south-west of France, towards the Pyrenees, a series of extraordinary caves have been discovered. Inside them, in what are known as the Ice Age Refuges, men, women and children lived and survived. At those latitudes, the summers were long enough to see grass grow on the plains and forests flourish in the sheltered valleys. Like the later hunter-gatherers of the north, the people of the Refuges gathered a wild harvest and hunted game. But, unlike the pioneers, they left a remarkable, stunning record of their lives.

Famously at Lascaux, in the steep-sided valley of the River Vézère, a tributary of the Dordogne, they painted on the walls of their caves. Some time around 15,000 BC, when a sterile Scotland froze in the grip of the ice, these people painted animals and occasionally themselves. At the entrance to the cave at Lascaux is a monumental representation of four huge aurochs bulls. Herds of wild horses, deer and bison thunder across the walls of the cave and, in all, more than 2,000 paintings were discovered. And they are not unique. On either side of the Pyrenees, 350 painted caves have been discovered and they date from between 30,000 BC to 8,000 BC.

They were painted by our direct ancestors. DNA testing has shown clear genetic links between the people of the Refuges and modern Scots. One of the most ancient Y chromosome lineages detected amongst Scottish men is known as M284 and it came from the cave painters. After 12,000 BC, when the ice began to retreat, bands of men and women began to leave the Refuges and travel north, probably following the herds of wild horses, deer and bison. Some of them walked into Britain. At that time, it was not an island but linked to continental Europe by a vast landmass. And their descendants kept moving north, ultimately bringing their genes, M284, to Scotland. About 6% of all Scottish men carry this living link to the Refuges, approximately 150,000 Scots. And it may well be that a proportion of Borderers and men living now in Hawick carry it. Perhaps the woodland clearers at Teviothead first brought the marker to Scotland where it has remained and flourished.

Prehistoric artefacts found around Hawick are not especially informative. Perhaps one of the earliest objects in the Hawick Museum and Gallery at Wilton Lodge Park is a stone hand axe (that is, an axe without a handle) lifted out of the Teviot. Fashioned from greywacke, a hard local stone, it was used for everyday functions such as chopping wood. Its edges will have been blunted by many centuries of clashing against the stones of the riverbed but greywacke is a coarse sandstone and, unlike flint or chert, cannot be sharpened to give razor-like blades. Arrowheads made from flint have been turned up by the plough in fields around the town and, in Wilton Lodge, there is a mysterious stone ball. It appears not to have been functional but symbolic or religious in some unknowable way. What these and a handful of other objects can tell us about prehistoric Hawick is meagre – a grey rickle of stones and bones.

What the cave paintings made by the ancestors of the pioneers who came to Scotland after the ice can say, by contrast, is vivid and striking. Human beings advanced northwards very quickly and will have reached the Tweed and Teviot valleys within only a few generations, while the memories and traditions of the paintings were still fresh. In essence, these people were pre-eminent amongst our ancestors, the earliest arrivals.

Perhaps the first and most obvious observation about the cave art of southern France and northern Spain is how technically brilliant it is. Working in darkness lit only by guttering torches, the painters gave life to the giant aurochs, the horses, the lions and the deer. Their mastery of form and colour far exceeded that of much of medieval European art and the lifelike animals gallop and leap across the rock walls, their movement often fully understood and realised. The techniques of perspective were not fully grasped until the Italian Renaissance of the 15th century and yet the cave painters had developed simple devices to give depth to their creations. Artistic intelligence of the highest level was at work in the damp and darkness of these underground galleries and the notion that prehistoric people were somehow primitive and deficient simply fades into the background, where it belongs. When Pablo Picasso visited Lascaux soon after the end of the Second World War, he was astonished by what he saw, remarking, 'We have learned nothing in 12,000 years.'

One of the most arresting images found in the caves is not that of an animal. As a form of signature, some prehistoric masters left a kind of stencil on the walls. Having filled their mouths with paint, they placed one of their hands flat on the rock surface and sprayed around it. It is a moving, direct link with a long past, our past. And it is also a long echo. When the great Italian painter, Raphael, was commissioned, patrons sometimes specified that the work should be done *con il suo mano*, 'with his own hand'.

Our ancestors also believed, as we do, that art was magical and sometimes best experienced alone. When archaeologists found the hidden entrance to the painted caves at Chauvet in southern France in 1994, they knew that they were the first to see them for 27,000 years. And they also discovered who had been the last to see the lost art of a disappeared culture.

Careful not to disturb the entrance to the cave more than was necessary, the excavators at Chauvet played arc lamps across the floor. And there, embedded in the clay, was a set of footprints. Small and only lightly indented, they were almost certainly the footprints of a boy, perhaps only ten years old. Two clay-stained handprints were also found on the cave wall and other, darker marks identified as charcoal told the archaeologists that the little boy had been carrying a torch. He wanted to see the magical mammoths and lions on the cave walls and it seems that he wanted to see them alone. And he was the last to see them before the cave faded out of memory and was lost.

When the descendants of the little boy began to leave the Refuges and walk northwards, more than one group ended their long journey in Scotland. In addition to M284, another marker from the people of the caves came to the Tweed basin and beyond. Much more rare, M26 is carried by only 12,000 Scotsmen, 0.5% of the modern population. But those few are amongst the most ancient inhabitants.

The final founding lineage first saw what was to become Scotland as a western horizon. They walked across the North Sea. At the height of the last ice age a massive ice-dome lay over northern Scandinavia. Its weight had the effect of pressing down on the Earth's crust to such an extent that it rose up in the ice-free south. Like a fat man sitting on a cushion, the part not under his backside is puffed up. Geologists call this a forebulge or isostatic lift. And so, when the ice crushed Scandinavia, what would later become the bed of the North Sea was squeezed up to become dry land.

Scientists have named this vast subcontinent Doggerland, after the Dogger Bank, and its lost geography is being slowly revealed. In their search for oil, the companies drilling in the North Sea have conducted intensive geophysical surveys and under the gravel, sand and silt they have found an Atlantis to the east. Flickering green images show river systems, a large inland sea called the Outer Silver Pit and a range of hills in the north that became the Dogger Bank. Ten thousand years ago some of our ancestors walked through this landscape to Scotland. And, when it was finally submerged, by 4,000 BC, more almost certainly sailed west to join them. They seem to us like ghosts now, men who walked out of the sea like selkies, but they were real enough and 20,000 Scotsmen are their descendants. The ancient marker of M423 is also found on the western shores of the North Sea, in southern Denmark and northern Germany.

These three markers, all of them Y chromosome markers traced through men and their sons, are the founding lineages of Scotland. Over millennia, many more would come but the pioneers from the painted caves and the lost plains and hills of Doggerland were the first to walk their lives under these northern skies, the first to paddle their curraghs up the Tweed and Teviot, the first to hunt in the wildwood and the first to gave the landscape names.

In the Borders, almost all of the names of our places are identifiably Celtic, English/Anglian or Scandinavian. Respectively, Kelso is from the Old Welsh *Calchvynydd* or 'Chalk Hill', Berwick from the Anglian *Berewich* or 'Barley Farm' and Selkirk from the Scandinavian *Seleskirkja* or 'Hall-Church'. These three groups of names were attached by politics, by people who followed each other into positions of power – powerful enough to confer names on places they controlled. But there exists a handful of much older names which have not changed with the times and seem to have come from the earlier peoples, perhaps out of the mouths of the pioneers.

River names are often ancient. On the east of Britain, several major rivers deriving from the same root word flow into the North Sea. They are the T-rivers. Thames is the most famous but Tain, Tay, Teviot and Tyne all appear to come from *ta*, a pre-Celtic word that meant something like 'to flow' or even 'to surge'. And Tweed and Ettrick are also very old (as is Cheviot) and no toponymist has ever explained their origins satisfactorily. Teviot is a name very like Cheviot but, past that facile observation, what else can be said? Slitrig is at least a little clearer. Originally the Old Scots *Slitterick*, it looks as though it is cognate to 'slitter', an excellent modern Border Scots term for something like 'liquid untidiness'.

In prehistoric – and historic – times, river meetings were significant places. Where Teviot meets Tweed at Kelso, the medieval town of Roxburgh was built in the shadow of a formidable royal castle and, on the opposite bank of the river, Scotland's wealthiest abbey was founded. But perhaps the most appropriate example is to be found near Peebles. On the haughland where the Lyne Water is joined by the Meldon Burn, there was a massive – and mysterious – enclosure formed by tree trunks set up as a stockade. It was built some time around 2,500 BC. Across the Lyne, on the plateau between it and the Tweed (just before the two join), was another significant place. Archaeologists have found the remains of ancient burial mounds from around 3,500 BC and there are also two standing stones and two cairns.

The Lyne ceremonial complex had great religious significance, no doubt, but it also stood at a strategic meeting place where three valley route ways converged. The confluence of the Slitrig and Teviot is very likely to have had a similar significance. Travellers from Liddesdale and the populous hill country to the south of Hawick could follow the Slitrig and meet people from upper and lower Teviotdale. The town has obliterated any prehistoric archaeology but the probability is that people have been greeting each other in the Sandbed and worshipping together near St Mary's for a very long time.

New lineages began to arrive in Scotland in the fourth millennium BC – this time carried by women. Mitochondrial DNA is passed on only by mothers through their daughters. Sons inherit it too but it dies with them. MtDNA markers J1B and J2a1 came originally from the east, the latter making its way across the European continent through the great river valleys of the Danube and Rhine before crossing what, by that time, had become the North Sea to Britain. And new ideas travelled with the new markers.

In Mesopotamia, the areas of modern Iraq and Syria once known as the Fertile Crescent, farming had begun to augment and then largely replace hunting and gathering as a means of producing food. Watered by the Tigris and the Euphrates and warmed by the Middle Eastern sun, land became farmland as people pioneered the cultivation of crops and the domestication of animals. Wild grasses were selectively harvested, with the largest and most calorific seeds being stored and then planted. Primitive wheat types such as emmer and einkorn evolved, as did a strain of barley. Other early crops included chickpeas, peas and lentils. Complementary to the growth of cultivation was the domestication of animals. Sociable, docile, manageable and meaty species were chosen and bred for their most useful characteristics. Most had two functions.

While only pigs were reared solely for their meat, cattle, goats, sheep and chickens could offer milk, wool and eggs as well.

Agriculture was largely women's work – or at least the humdrum, daily chores fell to them. While men looked after stock and ploughed (and hunted where possible), they weeded fields, harvested, winnowed and ground corn, milked cows, goats and sheep and collected eggs. It was an unequal division of labour that lasted in most farming societies until at least the 20th century.

Women, however, had another, vital interest in agriculture – it enabled them to have more children. In hunter-gatherer bands, infants took years to wean. Because adult human teeth capable of coping with most foodstuffs take a long time to develop, mothers had little option but to breastfeed their children for up to four years. There were no alternative foods available for their tender palates. And, while mothers are lactating, they are not so likely to conceive.

Cereal production changed these societal patterns radically. Ground cereal seeds could be made into a pappy porridge with animal milk that was suitable for weaning infants much earlier. The length of the birth interval was halved and farming populations quickly began to rise. This in turn forced emigration out of the Fertile Crescent and the techniques of farming began to ripple across the world, moving both east- and westwards.

Against this background, the arrival of two significant mtDNA markers in Britain after 4,000 BC is likely to herald the coming of farming. Women appear to have been the principal vehicles for the transfer of its techniques. This wave of migration shows that not only did new ideas move across the face of Europe, it seems that people did too.

Teviotdale and Tweeddale are amongst the most fertile agricultural regions in Britain. But the low-lying flat fields of the best farms along the banks of the rivers were not the sort of territory sought by the first to cultivate crops and domesticate animals in the Borders. Prehistoric perceptions of geography were different. Most low-lying, flat land was boggy and unusable. Free-draining areas were preferred, fields were small, sometimes little more than clearings or terraces or strips, and cultivation appears to have been possible in upland areas now wholly given over to stock rearing. In the fourth and third millennia BC, the weather seems to have been generally warmer and the growing seasons longer. Crops ripened at what seem now to be impossibly high altitudes.

Archaeologists often caution against generalising about what they call the accident of survival. The fact that prehistoric remains have been found in upland areas does not necessarily mean that these were premiated. It simply means that the ground has been less disturbed by ploughing and building than in the lowlands. Nevertheless, there is fascinating evidence of the way of life of early farmers and stockmen in an upland area immediately to the south of Hawick.

At Priesthaugh, where the road peters out and the hills rise steeply on all sides, the gossamer traces of a long past can be found amongst the heather and the coarse grass. In places such as this, it is possible to feel the quiver of time passing and, as the whaups wheel and cry, to sense the world turning. On the windy flanks of Burgh Hill, beyond the southern edges of Hawick Common, there stands a stone circle. No Stonehenge or Avebury, it is difficult to make out for most of the stones have fallen and some of those that have remained upright stand only a few centimetres in height. Originally, twenty-five stones had been set up in an elliptical egg-shaped arrangement and, judging by the churned clatch (mud) inside the circle, it probably enclosed a spring. The tallest stone has fallen but its 1.5 metre length can be made out in the mud.

Familiar only to the occasional walker and the farmer whose cattle graze around them, the half-forgotten stones of Burgh Hill were a place of central importance 5,000 years ago. A focus for the community who lived amongst the hills and deans between the Allan Water and the Dod Burn, it was holy, perhaps mysterious, a place of worship where long-lost rites were performed. Many circles or henges were built of wood with trimmed tree trunks packed into postholes and arranged in a circle, often organised by ancient geometry. Few vestiges of these remain but aerial photography has shown that some could be very large and impressive. At Dunragit, near Stranraer, three concentric wooden henges were identified and the largest covered six times the area of Stonehenge.

Burgh Hill's stones may not be monumental but they were well placed. Built on the 300-metre contour line, above a steeply shelving ridge sloping down to the modern road, the circle commanded wide views east towards Penchrise Pen, south to Gray Coat and Dod Rig, and behind it to the west rose the Burgh Hill. To the early peoples, horizons mattered and it is likely that, on the turning dates of the farming year, priests and worshippers will have looked for the sunrise over Penchrise Pen at particular points and at particular times. It may well be that the largest of the stones, at 1.5 metres, was aligned with one or more of these seasonal events.

Despite the fact that any sense of the nature of the ceremonies that took place inside the circle is impossible and unknowable, it is eloquent in other ways. Burgh Hill's little henge is a farmers' monument. It could only have been built by a substantial community who had settled in and taken ownership of one place. By its nature, farming involves sporadic, seasonal work and harvests at the end of it, which in turn, imply surpluses, at least temporarily. Properly managed and in good years producing a surplus, the agricultural cycle gave communities time, intervals between planting and reaping and in the winter, when they could do other work not related to food production. For hunter-gatherers, a project like the modest stone circle would not have been possible since there were too few of them and their way of life involved a near-constant need to find food.

The other substantial implication of the henge is the likelihood of a directing mind or minds. An individual, or perhaps a small group, directed the work needed to make the monument. They will have seen other henges elsewhere, understood something of the geometry needed, chosen the location and commandeered the workers required to drag the stones to the site and set them upright. Almost certainly a man, this person was a leader, probably a priestly lord who might also have conducted the ceremonies on the hillside – someone who combined what we would see as secular and spiritual roles. The distinctions we now make between Sunday and the rest of the week, between church and the rest of life are recent.

Most henges began as ditched enclosures. The central notion appears to have been the creation of a place apart from the world. With picks and baskets, work gangs dug circular ditches and on the upcast, drove in wooden posts to raise some sort of a screen. The ground at Burgh Hill is difficult to read but there may well have been an earlier ditch around where the stones now stand. The significance of the circle may also have been enhanced by the spring that still soaks the muddy ground. In any event, the effect was to make an emphatic division between inside and outside, between the observed, tangible world beyond the circle and the spiritual sphere of the gods inside it. The stones were intended as markers of exclusion, for at 16.6 metres at its widest diameter, they enclosed only a small area. Not everyone who lived around Burgh Hill could possibly be included – in fact, the idea may have been to preserve mystery by keeping out most people.

The farmers who did climb up the steep sides of the hill looked out over a landscape much changed. They and their ancestors had cleared the wildwood to make fields and pasture and, in their hands, they had held the tool that had helped them shape a new world. Wooden hefted, razor-sharp flint axes were swung to bring down trees, to trim boughs to make hurdle fencing, to help build homes and to chop firewood for heat and cooking. The early farmers owed a great deal to the axe and a symbol of their reverence for it was found in Hawick and is now held in the Royal Scottish Museum in Edinburgh.

A small, polished greenstone axe head was 'found in a garden in Hawick' in 1903 and immediately recognised as important. Greenstone is an igneous rock and the Hawick axe almost certainly came from the

Langdale Pikes in the Lake District. Near the summit ridges of this formidable range of mountains are the remains of prehistoric industry. Quarries of igneous rock were hacked out of the Pikes to win the stone needed to make these beautiful, darkly lustrous little axe heads. The debris from more than 75,000 has been found. Once the roughed-out shapes were brought down the mountainside, they were polished with abrasives to give them an attractive sheen. And then they began their journeys. All over Britain, Langdale axes have been found, many at prehistoric sites, and they show that, even as early as 4,000 BC, there were widespread trading networks all over Britain.

Too small and smooth to be practical, these objects probably symbolised the clearance of the wildwood, the creation of the fertile, food-providing patchwork landscape of early farming. They appear to have been acquired by powerful people and may have been hefted on to a wooden shank and held in ceremonies like a sceptre. The mystery and attraction of the Langdale axes probably came from their beginnings. Even though quarries of suitable stone could be easily found on the lower slopes of the Pikes, the miners preferred to climb up to the summit ridges and the highest deposits. In dangerous, rain- and windblown conditions, they fought the elements to bring down axes from these near-inaccessible places. Perhaps they believed that the highest rocks had been touched by the sky gods and had derived great power from them. In any case, one of these axes found its way into the grasp of a powerful individual who lived near the confluence of the Slitrig and the Teviot 5,000 years ago. Perhaps he was the directing mind behind a stone circle now lost beneath the buildings of Hawick.

Beliefs changed. Over the millennia following the erection of the circle at Burgh Hill, people gradually began to look elsewhere for their gods. Perhaps they did not have to look far. On the summit of Burgh Hill stand the contours of another, later prehistoric monument. Misleadingly known as hillforts and usually described as defences, there are several close to the old henge but none as impressive as the nearest.

Behind a massive rampart of two banks and two ditches, more than 8 metres broad, a large area of almost 2,000 square metres is enclosed. Set on the top of this singular hill that rises steeply between the narrow valleys of the Dod Burn and the Allan Water, this was a place of power – what archaeologists call a statement in the landscape. The grassed-over swales and hummocks of the ditches and banks will have looked very different in the first millennium BC. A stockade of stakes was usually driven into the banks (which stood much higher than they do now) and, seen from a distance, Burgh Hill hillfort will have looked formidable, glowering down from the summit.

On still days, observers will have also seen smoke rise from a large building inside the ramparts. Almost perfectly circular, foundations of what was once a roundhouse can be made out. The only dwelling in the hillfort, it must have been the residence of the man who commanded the area around. At 8.6 metres in diameter, it was a large house. Traces of a thick stone wall, more than a metre in width, are clearly visible. This probably rose to 2 metres in height and supported a conical roof formed by purlins resting on the wall head and lashed together at the apex. Thatched with bracken or turf, the roundhouse would be snug enough on the windy hill but very dark. The sole source of natural light was the doorway on the eastern side. Less than a metre wide, it was placed so that morning light could enter. Warmth, heat for cooking and a central focus were supplied by a downhearth – a circle of stones in the middle of the house. Some flat stones were usually intruded into the fireplace so that cooking vessels could be placed on them.

Roundhouses could be comfortable and clean but it was important to stay seated or lying when possible. There was no chimney or smoke hole (it would have let in the elements) and, on days without much wind, smoke from the central fire could collect in the cone of the roof. While occasionally splutteringly inconvenient, this tendency also acted as a safety measure. In the summer when the thatch was dry, sparks spiralling up from the downhearth were unlikely to set fire to the roof. Its design trapped a cone of carbon dioxide in the apex and immediately extinguished any sparks.

The firelit darkness of the roundhouse meant that much took place outside, especially anything that needed close work, like sewing or metalwork. Adjacent are the founds of a smaller hut, perhaps a store, and, on the other side, a scooped-out pit that might have been the location of a midden.

With only one house inside the hillfort and almost 200 metres of rampart to defend, this structure was no fort. Gates at either end would have made it difficult to repel any concerted attack. Instead, it is much more likely that Burgh Hill hillfort was a geographical, material expression of politics, a structure that required the labour of many to make it for a single individual. It almost certainly had a religious purpose as well. And there was the continuing issue of maintenance. No spring exists on Burgh Hill's summit and water would have to be carried up most days. Directly opposite the entrance to the roundhouse is an intriguing object. An earthfast rectangular stone, more than a metre high and 1.5 metres broad, looks manmade and it may have been somewhere the Lord of Burgh Hill stood or sat when his people gathered before him.

When silence was called for and the Lord of the Hill spoke, he will have used a Celtic language. By the first millennium BC, dialects of Old Welsh were spoken all over Britain, from Cornwall to Caithness, while Old Gaelic was the speech of the Irish. The landscape remembers the language of the builders of the hillforts and clearly visible from Burgh Hill is a name they will have used. Penchrise Pen is, in fact, a tautology and it means the 'Hill of Chrise Hill' – *pen* is Modern Welsh for 'head' and it is often used to describe a hill (Chrise sounds like a personal name and there is another hillfort on its summit). Named by the peoples of the first millennium, there are many 'pen' names in the Borders – Peniel Heugh, Pennygant Hill and Pennymuir are only three.

The Lord of the Hill rode out of the gates of his fort. In the late centuries BC, the Celtic society of Britain was an equestrian culture. The archaeological remains of horse gear (especially what are known as terrets, the metal links that hold a bridle or a halter together) and even of chariots have been found at sites all over the Borders. Lords and their warriors certainly rode to battle and what little is known of their weaponry suggests that they fought as light cavalry. Long slashing sabres have been found as well as the iron tips of lances.

These men supplied the military spine of authority in late prehistoric Britain. Much as the Highland clans did, kindreds controlled localities like the lands around Burgh Hill and they undoubtedly had links, perhaps alliances, perhaps enmities with their neighbours. The combination and recombination of kindreds in forming larger polities are impossible to follow in the absence of any documentary evidence or native records of any kind. In Ireland, a network of lesser kings, overkings and high kings existed and something similar may have evolved in Celtic Scotland. Later sources do attach territorial names to the map of Britain and these offer concrete but meagre clues.

The Selgovae were said to control the central Southern Uplands – that is, the Ettrick Forest, the Upper Tweed, Clyde and Annan, and Upper Teviotdale. To the east, in the Lothians, the Lower Tweed and the North Northumberland Plain, a people known as the Votadini were in control. But, along the watershed ridges of the Cheviots, where the modern border between England and Scotland now runs, the sparse picture becomes blurred. What appears to have been a large federation of kindreds, the Brigantes, held the Pennines and lands on either side. How far north did the reach of their kings extend? Beyond the Hexham Gap and into the Cheviots? It is impossible to be certain. In any case, the political map must have been redrawn from time to time. And it will not have resembled a modern map with firm borders, capital cities and so on. Webs of interlocking loyalties were what held federations like the Brigantes together – personal relationships between powerful men.

Hawick and its environs probably lay on the eastern margins of the territory of the Selgovae. The kindred name means something – it derives from the Celtic root *selg* for 'a hunt'. It seems to be a reference to an old way of life, how the hill peoples lived before the advent of farming. Stockmen by the first millennium BC, the Selgovae probably still hunted deer and other prey for meat. The names of people are often given to first contacts. For example, the vast area of Siberia is named after a small tribe who lived on its western edges. And 'the Hunters' may be how the Selgovae were described by the Votadinian farmers and ploughmen who were their neighbours and who followed a different culture.

In the landscape, the hunting methods of the hill peoples survive in place names. Chasing around the countryside on horseback after a fleeing fox or some other unfortunate creature with a pack of yowling dogs may be exhilarating but in the first millennium BC it would have been seen as a great waste of time and energy. Far more efficient was the old method of drive and sett. Usually in a defile or a place where geography made escape difficult, hunters would wait with bows, spears and nets. Beaters drove prey towards them, pushing the frightened deer, boar and many smaller creatures into what were known as 'elrigs' or 'eildricks' – *eileirg* is a Celtic root for a narrow valley or defile and, in the Craik Forest, the Eildrig Burn runs down Eildrig Hill past Eilrig Cottage and Eild Rig before joining the Borthwick Water. It remembers where the Selgovae, the Hunters, waited for the onrushing tide of terrified animals to reach the killing place.

Hawick's location on the margins between the territories of the Hunters and their neighbours, the Votadini, would become important later but, for the moment, in the middle of the first millennium BC, the focus shifts eastwards.

Ruberslaw makes a bridge between the uncertainties of late prehistory, the emphatic arrival of the Romans in the north, the period after their departure often called the Dark Ages and on into the religious politics of the 17th century. Its singular volcanic cone rises dramatically above Teviotdale and views from the summit are breathtaking on every side. This simple fact may have given the hill its name. Ruberslaw probably comes from Robbers' Law (although a credible alternative derivation is from an old version of Bedrule, a village owned by a woman with the Gaelic name of Bethoc, and it might have originally been the mouthful of Rulebethocslaw) and beacons lit on its top may have warned a wide area of the coming of raiders to the western Borders. Or its steep sides may have protected the stronghold of a nest of robbers, men who terrorised the countryside below.

A natural statement in the landscape, the hill attracted settlement around 500 BC and probably before then. The ascent is not arduous and Ruberslaw only becomes craggy and difficult at the summit. There, volcanic activity has formed a citadel with steep and rocky flanks and only very narrow, cleft-like entrances. The lower parts of the summit have 13–14 metre cliffs to defend them in most places. This was a hillfort that might have made military sense. That was certainly the view of a set of new arrivals in the Borders.

The Roman colonisation of England and Wales and, for short periods, parts of Scotland was very unusual because it was never driven by economics. Conquest was thought to be profitable – that was part of the point – and Julius Caesar became fabulously wealthy after his legions subdued Gaul. But what became the province of Britannia was believed to be impoverished, backward and rain-soaked by several commentators. Egypt, Asia Minor or Persia it was not. Not money but glory was what marched the legions northwards – the pressing need for military prestige by a succession of emperors. In AD 43, Claudius aimed to outdo Julius Caesar by actually conquering the place, showing that his power could reach across the much-feared Ocean (the name the land-loving Romans gave to the English Channel) and send his victorious armies almost to the ends of the Earth.

When Agricola began his governorship of Britannia, he was instructed by the Emperor Vespasian to move north in AD 79, almost certainly to bring the whole island into the Empire. At the beginning of their reigns, emperors' grip on power in Rome could be shaky and a blaze of military glory early on could stiffen resolve and strengthen loyalties. Vespasian knew he was dying and he wanted to ensure that the accession of his son, Titus, began in a positive atmosphere of expansion.

Military intelligence was much prized by Roman generals and, before a legionary could buckle on his breastplate, diplomats had been at work in the south of Scotland. Twenty years before, in a rebellion sparked by the Brigantes, it seems that the kings of the Selgovae had ridden south to swell the army of their fellow hill men. They were unlikely to be amenable to diplomatic blandishments and so, in classic divide-and-conquer fashion, the Romans allied themselves with the Votadini of the Lothians and the Lower Tweed and their legionary quartermasters probably made advantageous arrangements to buy Votadinian corn to supply the army.

In order to bottle up the hostile Selgovae, Agricola divided his invasion force, brigading the legions into two battle groups. From the fortress at Carlisle, the western group waded the Solway at low tide (a much safer passage than through the treacherous Solway Moss) and made their way northwards up Annandale. The eastern battle group set out from Corbridge on the Tyne, crossing the Cheviots a few miles east of the Carter Bar and marching towards the distant Eildon Hills.

When news of Vespasian's death reached Agricola, he halted the invasion to await orders from Rome and the new Emperor Titus. 'Onwards!' came the response and, by the end of the summer of AD 79, the legions were digging camps on the shores of the Firth of Tay. Behind them, a network of communications began to spread. To link Army Command North at York with the new naval base at Cramond, an arterial road was laid down. Dere Street can still be seen in the Cheviots near Ancrum and as it crosses Soutra Hill. A signal station was set up on Eildon Hill North and next down the line of sight to the south was Ruberslaw. On the summit citadel, excavators have found more than thirty dressed sandstone blocks cut in a Roman style and also a coin of the Emperor Vespasian.

Signalling was vital to the Roman army and, depending on contours and circumstances, several systems appears to have been used. Ruberslaw is approximately 11 miles south of Eildon Hill North and well beyond the range of the sort of semaphore used along Hadrian's Wall. In dull weather or darkness, beacons will have been lit and there is evidence that an elementary code was transmitted by making the fires flare and then damp down. On sunny days a large, polished metal surface could have been used in a similar way.

On 11 and 12 August 1948, a freak rainstorm devastated the Border country with six inches falling in only 24 hours. Damage was most severe in the lower Tweed as all of its upland tributaries rushed down to feed the spate in what would now be called a flash flood. Here is a contemporary newspaper report:

> The Tweed rose 17 feet. Nothing could stand against this rapidly rising torrent of water. Stock which had not had time to reach higher ground were swept away and drowned. Trees, shrubs, wooden buildings, fencing and other debris floated downriver, to be later piled up on the beaches as they reached tidal waters. Carcases of animals also lay there in numbers. So many bridges have been swept away – forty in Berwickshire and Northumberland alone – and many more have been rendered unsafe, that transport has been completely dislocated.

In the steep-sided valleys above Hawick, the roaring floods wreaked tremendous destruction but they did have at least one intriguing effect. Near the hamlet of Craik, now enveloped by one of the largest forests in Europe, the torrent tore away part of the left bank of the Borthwick Water and revealed a fascinating trace of a huge building project. It was a culvert built from carefully cut stone slabs expertly fitted together by highly skilled masons – 2,000 years ago.

When Agricola sent his battle groups in a pincer movement up Annandale in the west and across the Cheviots in the east, he aimed to surround the warlike Selgovae. But the metalled highways made in the wake of the legions did not separate these dangerous hill men from their southern allies, the Brigantes. And so, sometime after AD 79, a remarkable road was built to link the Annandale route with Dere Street as it ran north from near the Carter Bar to the Eildon Hills and beyond to the Forth. Traceable for 40 miles from the line of the modern A74, the road plunges into the great Craik Forest before emerging near Outerside Rig. It then appears to run down the haughland by the side of the Borthwick Water at least as far as Harden Bridge. And then the line of this massive piece of engineering disappears into the landscape.

In the popular imagination, Roman roads always ran arrow-straight but, in fact, surveyors usually took the easiest, most secure route in hilly terrain. They were also mindful of narrow places where ambushes could be set. The road did not simply stop at Harden and probably continued through the narrow defile below Borthaugh Hill before reaching Hawick and striking east by Wilton Lodge Park. Historians conjecture that the Roman builders pushed on down the Teviot and Tweed valleys all the way to the sea at Tweedmouth where a naval base probably guarded the estuary. A shadow of the ancient highway flits across the documents associated with Kelso's medieval abbey. Near Coldstream, the abbots' carts from Berwick used a stopover on the north bank of the Tweed at Simprim where it seems that an old road good enough for wheeled vehicles was still viable. In the reign of King Robert the Bruce, there is more than one mention of 'the Kingis Grate Rode from Annan to Rocesburg', the lost medieval city of Roxburgh that stood on the wide haughland opposite Kelso where it is enclosed by the Teviot and the Tweed.

Along the line of 'the Grate Rode' first built by Roman legionaries and auxiliaries are the clear remains of marching camps near the village of Denholm. These were dug as defended compounds for tents and bounded by a ditch and palisade to protect the work gangs from native warriors. Roman roads cut through existing farms, divided communities, disrupted free movement and created resentment. At

Minto kirkyard, evidence of the arrival of a foreign culture in the Borders was found when a Roman altar came to light.

As they do now, roads began with surveys. Once a line had been set by the *agrimensores* (land surveyors), work gangs began making a corridor through the landscape, cutting down trees and clearing scrub. Hundreds of soldiers will have been involved, each of them with well-honed skills as quarriers, labourers, carters, carpenters and masons, and others with a more martial role. The Craik road travelled through wild and inhospitable hill country that was full of danger. In the heart of the territory of the Selgovae, the road gangs will have needed protection from attack and ambush. As men cut down trees and dug trenches and drains, sentries will have searched the horizon for movement. Horse-riding warriors such as the Selgovae could suddenly erupt out of nowhere in a landscape they knew intimately.

Roman roads were usually 30 feet wide with a roadbed designed to accommodate wheeled vehicles such as oxcarts. Supplies as well as soldiers moved along the wide highway and, on occasion, will have had to pass each other. Because of the boggy and difficult terrain, the road builders sometimes dug down to the living rock or through banks of peat like railway cuttings. On each side of the Craik road, ditches ran and the upcast from these (and the spoil from the cuttings) was heaped on to the roadbed. And, beyond the ditches, a wide swathe of land was cleared to reduce the threat of ambush.

Culverts or drains like the one revealed by the floods of 1948 were cut across the road in places where the *agrimensores* reckoned water might pond. Once the culverts had been covered, a surface would have been rammed down. Gravel was used to metal the road and clear traces of this have been found. The highest point, the summit of this extraordinary feat of engineering, was Craik Cross Hill. Before the trees obscured it, the view from the road at this point must have been spectacular. Soldiers marching to Teviotdale and Dere Street could clearly see the Eildon Hills, what the Romans called *Trimontium*, and the signal station on the top of Ruberslaw. Behind them, to the west, the flat top of Burnswark Hill, Criffel beyond the River Nith and Skiddaw in the Lake District could all be made out. And, in places near this remote and wild viewpoint, several stretches of Roman metalling can be seen.

The great forest has obscured more than the view. Defended camps for the road builders must have been built at regular intervals but they cannot be detected by aerial photography until the trees are cut down. But when the landscape was clear 2,000 years ago, the visual impact of the road ribboning through the greens and browns of the hill country must have been arresting, an unequivocal statement that the empire had come north.

From the fort at Raeburnfoot, near Eskdalemuir, patrols will have reconnoitred in either direction and ridden out to protect slow-moving oxcarts as supplies ordered by legionary quartermasters moved east and west. The Roman postal system was famously fast and despatches from military commanders and letters were carried in the pouches of riders who could find remounts at regular intervals at forts along the roads. From the Antonine Wall between the Forth and the Clyde, messages could reach Rome in two weeks. It was not until the 19th century that communications again reached such a peak of efficiency.

The Craik Road was probably only in frequent use for a short time in the middle of the 2nd century when the empire temporarily included southern Scotland. Nevertheless, it remains a spectacular, if little understood or appreciated, Roman monument, a powerful link between what would become Hawick and an imperial past. In the settled, leafy tranquillity of Wilton Lodge Park, it is difficult to imagine the tramp and jangle of a cohort of Roman legionaries marching by the banks of the Teviot. But march that way they did and their ghosts are remembered up in the hills, in the green darkness of the Craik Forest. The faint outlines of their defended marching camps carry a silent memory of a different sort – the threat of the native warriors who watched them, these hated invaders who ignored obstructions and drove their roads through the conquered lands of the Selgovae kindreds, our ancestors.

When Rome decided to abandon the Antonine Wall around AD 157 and pull back to Hadrian's Wall, the legions still maintained a presence in the Borders. Forward forts garrisoned by scouts were established at Birrens in Annandale, Netherby on the Esk, Bewcastle in the high moorland to the east and at Risingham on Dere Street south of the Cheviot ranges. Patrols searched for trouble and intelligence but the Selgovae once again found themselves self-governing.

The province of Britannia lasted a long time and it was not until the beginning of the 5th century that the Roman Empire in the west began to disintegrate, leaving the cities of Britain to fend for themselves. Long before central administration imploded, the army in Britain had become both native and Germanic. Along the length of Hadrian's Wall, there is evidence that soldiering had become less formal and, in at least one of the great forts, there existed accommodation for families.

Important military commands may have become hereditary and the fascinating – and surprising – figure of Old King Cole was a shadowy presence, perhaps one of tremendously wide-ranging power. The nursery rhyme name is a curious survival and it comes from a late 4th-century general known as *Coel Hen* or Old Cole. In Latin, he was *Coelius* and probably the last to hold the office of *Dux Britanniarum*, the Duke of the Britains, meaning the four sub-provinces that comprised the former Britannia. *Coel Hen* will have commanded the sparse garrisons of Hadrian's Wall and, in the years following the withdrawal of the Roman imperial administration, his rule may have supplied some much needed stability and continuity. In the wake of withdrawal, the old Celtic kingdoms of Britain re-emerged, almost as though the Empire had never existed, and it is a measure of *Coel Hen*'s half-forgotten prestige that the dynasties of all of the northern kings claimed him as a progenitor. Sadly, no source called him merry or remembered his fondness for fiddle music.

The Celtic kingdoms of the north were not like more modern states – they had no fixed frontiers or a capital city, no records that have survived and only the most rudimentary administration. Rather, they depended on the raw power and military prowess of their kings and their war bands. Each kingdom was no more than a network of interlocking loyalties that could fluctuate quickly with events, expanding and shrinking almost like organisms.

The community who lived at the confluence of the Slitrig and the Teviot and in the sheltering hills around it lay in an area on the margins of at least four of these ancient kingdoms. To the south were the Brigantes, former allies of the Selgovae and a federation which appears to have split into its constituent parts. Most famous of these was the kingdom of Elmet around the modern city of Leeds.

To the west stretched the great Solway kingdom of Rheged. Hinged and based on the old Roman city of Carlisle and the fortresses at the western terminal of Hadrian's Wall, its king inherited some of the afterglow of the Empire. Not only were the forts and the wall largely intact, Roman Carlisle still functioned as a city. As late as the end of the 7th century a municipal water supply continued to flow and fountains sparkled and, even in the 12th century, chroniclers reported that Roman buildings with Latin inscriptions could be seen and the medieval inhabitants of Carlisle walked on paved streets.

The greatest king of Rheged was Urien and his name derived from *Urbgen*, meaning 'born in the city'. From Stranraer in the farthest west, his realm reached along the Solway coast to Urien's birthplace at Carlisle and, from there, turned southwards at least to Penrith and probably down into Lancashire beyond. How far Urien's warbands could ride in safety up the Esk and Ewes valleys and into the hills is unclear. The ancient territory of the Selgovae is likely to have retained a measure of independence if only because it was so difficult for outsiders to control (including the Roman legions in their pomp) and, as hill country, probably not thought to be worth the effort.

To the east of what became Hawick lay the lands of the Gododdin, a kingdom that left an atmospheric sense of itself in epic poetry, and another, smaller, realm that is now little more than a name and a shadow. Like Rheged and Brigantia. Gododdin understood itself in Old Welsh, the same language spoken in prehistory by the peoples who named Penchrise Pen and many other places in the Borders. Perhaps Peebles is the best known and it comes from *pybyll*, a word meaning 'tents' or 'shelters' and it is likely a reference to shielings by the Tweed.

From their citadels on Edinburgh's Castle Rock, Traprain Law in East Lothian, probably Eildon Hill North and Yeavering Bell near Wooler, the Gododdin kings ruled over rich swathes of fertile farmland. And they were wealthy. In 1919, a huge hoard of Roman silver was found on the summit plateau of Traprain Law. Buried beneath what turned out to be the floor of a roundhouse were more than a hundred items – silver cups, tableware, spoons, bowls and coins. Some of the larger pieces had been cut up and folded over. This was bullion rather than fine art, its value reckoned by weight and probably a tribute payment made in the dying years of the Roman Empire in the west.

Closer to the eventual site of Hawick was another polity based on an imposing fortress. *Calchvynydd* is the Old Welsh name for Kelso and it means 'Chalk Hill', a reference to a chalky outcrop on the west bank of the Tweed. But it seems that there was a territory, perhaps a small kingdom, also known as *Calchvynydd*. Its ruler may have held court not in Kelso but across the river at the extraordinary eminence of Roxburgh Castle. This great medieval stronghold has a long history, and historians believe that from it a warband controlled a triangular area between the Tweed and the Teviot (the rivers join very close to the old castle) that extended westwards to the line of Dere Street, the Roman road running from the Cheviots to Trimontium near Melrose.

In an epic poem composed some time after AD 600, a ruler known as Catrawt of Calchvynydd rode out of his fortress at the head of his warband to join the host of the kings of the Gododdin. Neither he nor his warriors would return.

Turning points in history are rarely seen as such by those who lived through them. In the everyday confusions of advances and reverses, gains and losses, the flow of history can be hard to discern. But the battle fought in 600 by the Gododdin kings and their allies was different. Catrawt and his cavalry rode south from the Tweed Valley to Catterick in North Yorkshire. The cataracts or the rapids on the River Swale gave the place its Roman name, *Cataractonium*, and, over fifteen centuries, it has changed only a little. Above the fast-flowing river stood a large Roman fort, not far from the modern army camp. As now, it was a strategic place, pivotal on the great north road of Dere Street and also close to a junction with the road over the moors to the western, Cumbrian coasts. It was the place where a bloody battle would be joined.

For at least 150 years and probably more, Germanic warriors had been sailing the North Sea to settle in eastern Britain. According to the scholar and historian Bede of Jarrow, the Angles established a kingdom on the rock at Bamburgh in 540. These were men from Angeln, an area of southern Denmark and western Germany north of the Elbe. Historians believe that much of their low-lying land was inundated, forcing communities to cross the North Sea and find new homes. Ida was said to have been the first king to rule from Bamburgh and he may have dignified what had been a stronghold of piratical raiders. In any event, the Angles joined with the native Celtic Bernicians and formed a powerful alliance that began to threaten the surrounding kingdoms, Gododdin in particular. With the Anglians of Deira, in modern Yorkshire, the Germanic incomers presented a formidable new political force.

Led by Yrfai map Golistan, Lord of Edinburgh, the allied army of the native kings were utterly defeated on the banks of the Swale. Amidst great slaughter, few of the Celtic host survived. But the bard, Aneirin, lived to tell a tragic tale of the defeat of Gododdin and the fall of the rulers whose halls stood on the rocks of Traprain, Edinburgh, Yeavering and Eildon Hill North.

By 603, Aethelfrith, the King of the Bernicians, had destroyed another Celtic army, this time commanded by Aedan macGabrain, King of Argyll. It seems that the men of the west had been raiding in the Tweed Valley and the Bernicians caught up with them in Lauderdale, at Addinston, where the ditches of a tremendously impressive fort can still be made out on the summit of the prominent ridge. By 637, the Gododdin citadel on Edinburgh's castle rock had fallen and most of the south-east was in Anglian hands. In the centuries that followed, language, culture and place names would all change and Hawick would emerge from the mists of history.

3

AYE DEFEND

HAWICK IS AN English name. After the victories at Catterick in 600 and Lauderdale three years later, the warbands of the English-speaking kings at Bamburgh were overrunning Tweeddale and Teviotdale. They called their realm Bernicia and it was derived from *Bernaccia* or *Bryneich*, Old Welsh names that meant the 'Land Between the Hills', probably a reference to the lower Tweed. To the north of the great valley, the Lammermuirs rise and to the south the Cheviots mark a definite barrier. The Bernicians came to control the area around Hawick and, some time after their warbands had swept aside native opposition as far as the Lothians and the Forth, they gave the place its name.

Hawick literally means 'Hawthorn Farm'. In Old English, the first element comes from *Haegathorn* and, because the spikey little bushes and trees make a good barrier, they were often used for hedging. An alternative old name was 'Quickset', a recognition that it was fast growing, a valuable characteristic for a means of defining the ownership and management of land. By extension, Hawick is often said to mean 'Hedge Farm'.

This disappointingly prosaic derivation is coloured by links to the spiritual world. Boundaries could be magical and *haegathorn* is cognate to *haegtesse*, 'a woman who had prophetic powers', and, incidentally, a name that has come down to us as 'hag'. These women could cross boundaries between the observed, real world to the unseen, spirit world – the other side. *Haegzusa* were spirits sometimes known as 'Hedge Riders'.

The Bernician warbands were pagans in the early 7th century and magic mattered to them. When they converted to Christianity, the power of the hawthorn endured. Not only was Christ's crown of thorns thought to be made from it but the Burning Bush was also popularly seen as a hawthorn. In a story once widely believed by early Christians, Joseph of Arimathaea, Jesus's uncle, came to Britain soon after the crucifixion. With him he carried the Holy Grail, a cup used by Christ at the Last Supper and by those who knelt at the cross to collect drops of the Holy Blood. The Grail has passed into endlessly recurring legend but Joseph was believed to have done something else of great moment. When he planted his staff in the soil of Wearyall Hill near Glastonbury, said to have been the first Christian church in England, it grew into a hawthorn tree, the Holy Thorn. For many centuries, cuttings have been taken and the offspring of the ancient tree grow all over England near many churches.

The legend of Joseph of Arimathaea is late but the association of hawthorns with holy places is not. The bushes and trees had a more practical function in the past (and now) and it makes a fascinating link. At the bottom of ditches such as those dug around the summit of Burgh Hill and Penchrise Pen, it was common to plant hawthorns. Once they had begun to flourish, the plants presented a prickly, discouraging obstacle to animals as well as people. Does this use of hawthorn suggest another extended meaning for the name of Hawick – 'Defended Farm'?

St Mary's Church is clearly ancient. Its fabric was rebuilt in 1763 on the foundations of a much older building, probably the medieval parish church. There are two tombstones in the graveyard dating to the 17th century. After a fire in November 1881, St Mary's was again rebuilt and only the tower remains from 1764. So far, so unexceptional. What is intriguing and what attests to a great age for the church is its location and the very obvious mound it sits on.

In the earliest centuries of Christianity in the Near East, communities known as the Desert Fathers began to form. They were essentially hermits, devout men who had fled from the cities, the threat of Roman persecution and what a much later Borders abbot would call 'the tumult of the world'. The Desert Fathers often lived harsh lives in caves in the wastes of Sinai and Syria and later built simple cells near sources of water. These men sought solitude, places where they would be left in peace to pray, contemplate and try to reach states of spiritual perfection. Nearness to God, eternal life at His right hand and a complete understanding of the meaning of life and death were their goals. And an ascetic, hard existence in the fierce heat of the desert was thought to be purifying.

The Desert Fathers were enormously influential in the foundation of western monasticism. Early communities of monks were established at liminal places such as Iona and Lindisfarne, physically apart from the tumult of the world and where earth, water and sky met in an elemental celebration of the glory of Creation. In place of the endless sands of the Sinai and Syrian deserts, the sea (and for inland foundations, rivers) would surround them and the winds and winter storms would purify. When Aidan was invited to come from Iona by Bernician kings to set up a new monastery on the royal estate at Old Melrose in the middle of the 7th century, he chose for its site a loop in the course of the Tweed near Bemersyde. The river peninsula was closed off by a vallum, a ditch dug by the monks to mark off the holy ground of their community from the secular world beyond it. Such ditches existed around many early monasteries and, at Iona, the vallum can still be clearly seen.

Aidan's choice began a persistent tradition in the Borders. The later medieval abbeys at Kelso, Dryburgh and Jedburgh were all built on the sites of much earlier churches in the loop of rivers and their landward precincts marked off by a ditch. These magnificent churches were all, incidentally, dedicated to St Mary. Perhaps a cult of the Virgin was especially powerful in Tweeddale and Teviotdale.

At Hawick, St Mary's stands in a loop of the Slitrig, very close to where it meets the Teviot. This a defined area, bounded on three sides by water, as at Old Melrose. All traces of an enclosing ditch have been erased by the buildings and streets of the modern town and no archaeologist has looked for one. But it may well be there, hidden under Hawick.

St Mary's mound encourages the possibility of an ancient church. Sacred places were not always destroyed or ignored during the era of Christian conversion – they often retained their status as focal points. In fact, papal advice to missionaries was pragmatic. If it aided the process of bringing the people to God and smoothed the transition from pagan beliefs, then worship should take place where temples, stone circles or shrines stood and eventually many churches were built inside their sacred ditches and the old henges. Conversion usually began with the leaders of a pagan society, lords and kings, and these men may well have had a priestly role as well as temporal, political power. In a real sense, the temples or precincts belonged to them and, if they sanctioned their use for Christian worship, it was an act that supplied all sorts of legitimacy.

All over Britain, churches show signs of having been built inside ditching, on raised areas and in places where prehistoric artefacts have been found. The beautiful church at St Vigeans, near Arbroath, is a good example. Not only does its mounded site resemble St Mary's, it has produced an array of fascinating archaeology from the Bronze Age to very beautiful Pictish symbol stones. Such continuity can be observed in other, less obvious ways.

Noticed by the famous 18th-century naturalist and clergyman, the Rev. Gilbert White of Selborne in Hampshire, very many churches have yew trees in their churchyards. Every part of the yew is poisonous and it was thought that they were planted to ward off animals that might dig up recent burials or otherwise desecrate the graveyard. However unlikely that may be, the fact is that yews often live to very great ages and some are much older than the churches they were thought to be protecting. The famous example at Fortingall in Perthshire was 4,000 years old. Now, yews were sacred in pagan beliefs and it is certain that the oldest still living predate the arrival of Christianity. It follows that those churches with ancient trees in their churchyards were built on the sites of pagan temples.

When the word of God began to be spoken in the Borders, it had come from the west. Christianity flourished at first in the towns and cities of the Roman Empire (pagan is from *paganus* which originally meant 'a country man') and there is strong evidence for an early church in Carlisle, perhaps even as early as the mid 4th century. It is in the nature of the church to proselytise, to reach out and make conversions and there is unshakable, concrete evidence for the reach of Christian belief up the Liddel Water at a very early date.

Flooding once again revealed the remains of the long past. Near Newcastleton in Liddesdale, where the Ralton Burn joins the Liddel Water, a winter spate in late 1933 toppled a drystane dyke on the riverbank. Built into it was an ancient tombstone and a shepherd noticed a large stone with what looked like writing on it lying in the riverbed. It carried the Christian formula *Hic iacit Caranti Filii Cupitani* or 'Here lies Carantus, son of Cupitianus' and the style of the inscription places its carving in the 5th century. In a British context, far less a Scottish, this is very early indeed, long before the foundation of Iona or Lindisfarne. And it shows Christianity moving eastwards from Carlisle and probably continuing up over the watershed hills. If conversion did indeed flow in this direction – and as early as the 5th century – then Hawick lay directly in its path. The discovery of very early Christian inscriptions at Peebles and the Yarrow Valley encourage the notion of spread and perhaps Christians have worshipped on the mound at St Mary's for a very long time.

The second element in Hawick's name is much less ambiguous and nothing to do with ephemeral notions of spirituality. In Old English, *wick* meant 'a farm', almost certainly with the sense of an outlying farm. Berwick is a place name of the same sort and date. It means 'Barley Farm' and *wick* was used all over England and southern Scotland to mean an outlying farm attached to a royal or aristocratic estate. Famous examples of this type of name can be found in the south at Gatwick ('Goat Farm') or Chiswick ('Cheese Farm'). Much closer to home is Borthwick and it means 'Byre Farm', probably a reference to stock rearing rather than cereal production. Other names support this. Borthwick Mains is in the valley of the Borthwick Water while in the higher country immediately to the north is Borthwickshiels. This was where herdsmen summered out in rudimentary shelters as their herds and flocks grazed the high pasture and the lowland fields were rested and some cultivated for crops. Darnick, near Melrose, meant 'Hidden Farm', perhaps somewhere screened by trees. Hawick has retained its 'w' in spelling if not pronunciation while Darnick has lost it in both senses.

Where was the centre of the royal estate that included the Hawthorn Farm or Hedge Farm as an outlier? This is a complex question and one that centres around the introduction of the shire organisation to the Borders by its new Bernician overlords. Before these conquerors removed native Celtic aristocrats, land was organised into estates known as *maenorau*. There is one near-perfect survival in the Manor Valley near Peebles and its very defined territory was administered by an official known as the *Maer* (which gave rise to the later *Mormaer*, 'mayor' and a Scottish surname) from a central point and also, as Christianity was increasingly adopted, from a central church.

The Bernicians may simply have taken over the maenorau and renamed them shires but they also introduced two new names for those who ran royal estates on behalf of the king. The principal official was a *thegn* or 'thane' and a lesser, more obligated individual was known as a 'dreng'. These men paid what was later known in Scots history as *feu-ferme*, a money rent for land, and were obliged to do seasonal ploughing for the king. Often they also had to cut wood and do carting work as well as give an annual tribute of livestock. All of this was known as boon-work. Sometimes thanes and drengs were compelled to provide hospitality for the king and his warband. Because food rents were perishable and, apart from livestock, not easy to transport in bulk, the royal retinue moved around to consume all that was owed to the king by those who ran his estates for him. That this system of land management was common around Hawick there can be no doubt for a dreng left the name of his status on the landscape.

North of the town, below Drinkstone Hill, lies the farm of Drinkstone. It is a very old settlement with an immense continuous history – more than a millennium – because the name derives from *Dreng's Tun*, the 'Dreng's Farm'. And a short distance to the east, the Boonraw Burn flows through West Boonraw and then East Boonraw, a clear memory of the obligatory boon work done on behalf of the dreng at Drinkstone. It is a remarkable survival and these names by themselves suggest a Bernician shire in Teviotdale that included Hawick.

Significantly smaller than modern shires, these old estates were sometimes still to be found on recent maps as late as the 19th century. North Northumberland contained Norhamshire, Islandshire (the mainland opposite Lindisfarne), Bedlingtonshire and, over the Tweed, the shadows of Scottish examples have been traced by the great medieval historian, G.W.S. Barrow. In his collection of essays published as *The Kingdom of the Scots*, Professor Barrow establishes that shires had mother churches, what he called *ecclesiae*. This Latin term had been borrowed into Old Welsh and he argued convincingly that, when it was attached to churches, they predated any Bernician foundation and were pre-eminent. *Ecclesia* became Eccles in Berwickshire, Eccles Cairn near Yetholm, Eaglescairnie in East Lothian and even Gleneagles in Perthshire.

Jedburgh was reckoned by Barrow to be the focus of a Bernician royal estate and, if the 'eccles' name has disappeared or was never applied, there is archaeology to support its importance as a mother church. The remains of no less than five 8–10th-century crosses have been found in and around the town and parts of a beautiful stone shrine, at least five feet long and three feet high, have also been uncovered. This group of objects can be conjectured into a pattern. Such an elaborate and beautifully made shrine, complete with decorations known as vine scrolls and birds, almost certainly housed the bones of a saint. Perhaps it was St Cuthbert. After the Viking attacks on his shrine at Lindisfarne in 793, monks carried his bones around the north where they rested at various inland locations, well away from danger. Perhaps they lay at Jedburgh. The findspots of the five crosses suggest them as waymarkers for pilgrims – a set of physical signs that they were entering a place of great holiness where even the ground itself was sacred.

What is certain is the existence of Jedburgh as an important ecclesiastical centre before 830. In that year, Bishop Ecgred of Lindisfarne ordered a new church to be built at what his scribes called *Gedwearde* (or *Jedworth*). The second element of the name has been replaced by burgh but it meant an enclosure, perhaps a sacred precinct. Here is the entry in the chronicle of Symeon of Durham that describes what the bishop ordained:

> Ecgred, Bishop of Lindisfarne, bestowed upon the holy confessor, Cuthbert, that vill [of Norham] with two others which he had founded, [both] called by the same name, Jedworth, with their appanages.

There is a great deal in this short passage. By bestowing lands on Cuthbert, the bishop intended the church of St Cuthbert and may also have meant that Cuthbert's church had founded two churches at Jedburgh. But it is the use of the word 'appanages' that denotes a large estate. These stretched from Dune (the Dunion) to Teviotmouth (presumably at Kelso) and thence beyond the mountain eastwards. This is obscure but another version of the entry talks of the two Jedburghs, to the southern district of the Teviot. Leaving aside the difficult question of more than one Jedburgh, the appanages of the church of the shrine and the pilgrim crosses clearly had extensive lands to the south of the Teviot. It may well be that Hawick was included in this estate as an appanage – what Scots lawyers would later call a pendicle – to a royal estate based at Jedburgh. And the dreng at Drinkstone may also have been attached.

Well into the Middle Ages, Teviotdale was seen as a distinct ecclesiastical entity and part of the great estates of the church of St Cuthbert – what was known as the *Terra Lindisfarnensis*. When the saint's shrine was moved from its remote island home to Durham and a great cathedral was built, Durham continued to claim Teviotdale as part of its estates.

In the 8th century, defined frontiers mattered as much as they do now and immense labour went into making them emphatic. One of the greatest manmade monuments in Europe is Offa's Dyke. Built at the behest of the great Mercian king who reigned between 757 and 796, it was raised to mark the boundary between his Midland kingdom and the kingdoms of Wales. At 150 miles in length, this frontier was impossible to patrol or defend except at strong points but it did have one major inhibiting effect. The reiving of cattle was common and Offa's military planners reckoned that a substantial dyke (it is 19.8 metres broad and 2.4 metres high at its greatest extent and will have been much higher when first dug) with its parallel deep ditching would at least slow down the movement of stolen beasts. And the massive presence of the Dyke – much longer than either the Antonine Wall or Hadrian's Wall – left no doubt about who was on the wrong side.

After his signal victory at Addinston in 603, Aethelfrith and his Anglian warbands began to colonise the Borders, pushing native kings further and further westwards. And it seems that a frontier was finally agreed. The Catrail was like Offa's Dyke in that it had a similar, although more modest, arrangement of ditching and banking and it was considerably shorter at about 60 miles in length. It ran from Torwoodlee, north of Galashiels, and up the Yarrow Valley before turning south across the hills to the Borthwick Water. From there it struck into the hill country south of Hawick before reaching Peel Fell and petering out at the foot of the western ranges of the Cheviots. The Catrail may well be a very early witness to an enduring Borders pastime – the reiving of cattle.

Its 60-mile length appears to mark a boundary between Anglian Tweeddale and Teviotdale and the Old Welsh-speaking kingdoms in the upcountry to the west. Place names seem to support this supposition. To the west are many more Old Welsh names like Ettrick Pen, Peebles, Berrybush and others while to the east lie the Anglian names of the likes of Hawick, Selkirk, Midlem and more. The distinction is not uniform or exclusive. Kelso is an Old Welsh name and Langholm is Anglian but the generality holds good.

The Catrail places Hawick firmly in an Anglian atmosphere and the examples of Drinkstone and Boonraw encourage the sense of a landscape organised in shires. It was a tremendously durable administrative entity lasting thirteen centuries before local government was reorganised in 1974. Into the 11th century, the Catrail may indeed have been seen as marking the western extent of the vast holdings of the Bishops of Durham. Drengs and thegns are mentioned regularly in the sparse documents of the medieval Border country until the 12th century and beyond and the land they cultivated seems to have belonged to the king or at least a powerful, more local lord, perhaps a bishop.

It is highly unlikely that the takeover of Teviotdale and Tweeddale by Anglian warbands in the 7th and 8th centuries had much immediate effect on ordinary people – the farmers who coaxed a living from the land. There were, no doubt, new names and faces but, since the value of land resided in what it could produce, no sensible incomer would do anything much to prejudice productivity amongst his tenants. While the new overlords largely decapitated the native Celtic aristocracy or drove them away, their numbers were unlikely to have been large, certainly not in the early period of takeover. As late as the 13th century, Thomas of Ercildoune (modern Earlston), better known as

Thomas the Rhymer, was collecting stories from Old Welsh speakers in the Borders, a shrivelling speech community that appeared to survive in upland and isolated areas.

Over what was probably a lengthy period, the colonising Angles did change the culture of cultivation. Small Celtic fields (of the sort still seen in the west of Ireland) were replaced by the ox-gang, a long and narrow layout that allowed a heavy ox-drawn plough to go as far as it could before the lie of the land forced a turn. This was done in a necessarily wide angle when the team was brought around. Aerial photography is good for detecting Anglian ox-gangs and the characteristic S-shape is often clearly visible – caused by the wide turn of the slow-moving oxen.

The Angles laid out villages in the Borders. Midlem, originally Middleham, is a good example and the modern houses are built on the footprints of the old. Arranged around a triangular green, the rows of cottages have long ox-gangs behind them. Under a dusting of early winter snow the shape of the old fields can clearly be made out. Other villages, like Lilliesleaf, were simply single streets.

Anglian Hawick is difficult to visualise. The modern town centre obscures it entirely. Did it lie inside the area bounded by the Slitrig and the Teviot? Only archaeology will answer this central conundrum but, if there had indeed been a well-defined and well-defended enclosure protected by hawthorn and a ditch to the west, then it would make every sort of sense to site houses inside it. The earliest trace of building in Hawick is the Mote and it is likely to have been placed close to the area of prime settlement in the 12th century. Perhaps Hawick's single street extended from near the Mote (defenders discouraged building too close to castles, even small ones) down towards St Mary's Church. Where Drumlanrig Square now widens, there existed Auld Mid Raw, certainly a very old group of thatched and rubble-built cottages. Demolished in the 19th century, it was the survivor of what seems to have been a two-street arrangement. Auld Mid Raw was flanked by Back Raw and

Fore Raw – all of which sounds very like the contours of the original Anglian settlement. Hawick probably only crossed the Slitrig when Drumlanrig's Tower was built, probably in the 16th century. The oldest part of the fortification dates to the 1550s although traces of an earlier building have been conjectured.

If the original village ran downhill from the Mote to St Mary's, the backlands will have been relatively short, each set stopping short at the banks of the Slitrig or Teviot. If Fore Raw and Auld Mid Raw lay on either side of a street (Back Raw's name discourages the notion of it forming part of a main thoroughfare), that will have been the location of Hawick's earliest market.

Where Drumlanrig Square now meets The Loan stood Hawick's old West Port. Pulled down in 1762, it guarded the main road from Langholm and Carlisle and part of its founds can still be seen between 16 Drumlanrig Square and 2 The Loan. Also known as the Townhead Port, its location reinforces the sense of the earliest settlement lying to the west of St Mary's and its mound.

As often in Hawick, cherished traditions echo history. The term *guitterbluid* is technically not a flattering one with its original meaning of something like 'a guttersnipe' but it is, in fact, a description claimed with pride by a select few and celebrated in verse:

Through shade or shine
The Guitterbluid sin syne
Has circled roond the green auld Moat.

The definition is clear. Only those born 'between the two rivers', between Slitrig and Teviot, can call themselves *guitterbluids*. And far more than being mere Westenders, there is a clear sense of them being original – the descendants of the first people to live in Hawick.

The location of the earliest East Port is much less obvious. Since it would have stood at the river crossing, ford or bridge, it was likely to have been on the banks of the Slitrig, lying somewhere between St

Mary's and the Sandbed. Whatever the precise place, it was overlooked by the church and its mound.

At the same time as the early settlers came to Hawick, a great saint saw a vision from the hills above Melrose. In the Year of Our Lord 651, a young man and his dogs were guarding their flock at the summer shieling, watching for wolves, making sure none of his sheep strayed. As gloaming shaded into night, the young shepherd was woken, his sleep broken by bright lights in the sky far to the east. Shafts of celestial glory carried uncountable ranks of angels. They had come for Aidan, the bishop of God's church on the holy island of Lindisfarne, and they would raise him up from the shores of the North Sea to sit at God's right hand.

Cuthbert's life was changed utterly by his vision and, soon after, he rode to the abbey at Old Melrose, in the loop of the Tweed, to take holy orders. After an exemplary life, he too was raised up to sainthood and a cult soon developed around his miracles and his preaching. An early and anonymous life of Cuthbert makes much of his persuasive abilities as a preacher and, in his great work *The Ecclesiastical History of the English People*, Bede elaborates. The native peoples of the Borders were almost certainly already Christians but those in the new Anglian settlements in Teviotdale were not:

> He used mainly to visit and preach in the villages that lay far distant among high and inaccessible mountains, which others feared to visit and whose barbarity and squalor daunted other teachers. Cuthbert, however, gladly undertook this pious task, and taught with such patience and skill that when he left the monastery [at Old Melrose] it would sometimes be a week, sometimes two or three, and occasionally an entire month, before he returned home, after staying in the mountains to guide the peasants heavenwards by his teaching and virtuous example.

From Melrose, it sounds as though Cuthbert rode west, perhaps to the new village at Hawick, perhaps further into the hills behind. The great cathedral at Durham was later built on Cuthbert's bones and, soon after his death, churches were dedicated to him, the saint of the North, of the glittering kingdom of Northumbria.

Bede's *Life of St Cuthbert* talked of his expeditions from the monastery at Old Melrose into the hills of the Borders. The conversion of pagans – *pagani* or 'country people' – was his mission and tradition holds that he built a hermetical cell on the knowe St Mary's now stands on. If that was more than simply tradition, it would certainly accord with the habits of the Desert Fathers, the Near Eastern monks so admired by Cuthbert and his contemporaries.

The medieval chronicler, Reginald of Durham, wrote of a miracle witnessed in Cuthbert's more modest church near Hawick. Founded in 687, the year of the saint's death, this chapel stood on the banks of the 'Slitrith' and soon became a focus for pilgrimage. Two devout women, Saegifa and Rosfritha, came to Cuthbert's church and, when the altar candle faltered, another miraculously took its place 'which diffused all round its beaming rays'.

The site of this ancient chapel was probably at Cogsmill below the farm at Adderstonesheils. In 1830, trees were planted to mark the holy ground and the area around was known as Chaipel Park. But perhaps the most significant aspect of Reginald's story was that he noted the home of Saegifa and Rosfritha. They had come from 'Hawic' to worship on the banks of the 'Slitrith'. If the tale is to be trusted, it plots a very early date for the existence of the village of Hawick – the last quarter of the 7th century – and it names the first people – the first Teris. Not only does their village have an Anglian name but so too do Saegifa and Rosfritha. The first element of the latter is cognate to the more common names of Rosalind or Rosamund and *frith* means 'friend'. Rosfritha may mean something like the oddly appropriate 'horse friend'.

The world they lived in has been submerged beneath modern architecture and modern agriculture but much of it can be conjectured, even reconstructed, by analogy. The background to the arrival of the Angles in the Borders is perhaps surprising. Rome and the glory that it was left their marks on the landscape and influenced the incomers deeply. As fellow conquerors of the Old Welsh-speaking natives, the farmers who tilled the fields and tended beasts arrogated to themselves imperial Roman titles and ceremony, whoever was in charge. On royal progresses around Northumbria, its kings understood the importance of show, of displays of power to the conquered and how important it was to borrow Roman grandeur. It granted legitimacy and added the shadow of greatness. Here is the eminent historian, Bede of Jarrow, writing about King Edwin, the ruler of Teviotdale and Northumbria in the 620s:

> So great was his majesty in his realm that not only were banners carried before him in battle, but even in time of peace, as he rode about amongst his towns, estates and kingdoms with his thegns, he always used to be preceded by a standard-bearer. Further, when he walked anywhere along the roads, there used to be carried before him the type of standard which the Romans called a tufa and the Angles call a tuff.

The *tufa* was a clear signal that the Northumbrian kings saw themselves as the inheritors of the empire – the successors of Rome. So extensive was their military and political reach by the early 7th century that they called themselves *Bretwaldas* – 'Britain rulers'. The importance of this was the use of the name of Britannia, the old Roman province, to denote their wide sphere of influence. Old place names remember that, for once in our history, power did not lie in the south but the north. The name of Mercia, the kingdom of Offa, is cognate to the word 'marches' and it was originally applied to mean the southern borders of Northumbria. Similarly the old term for the districts of the lower Tweed Valley and much of fertile Berwickshire is the *Merse* – the 'northern marches of Northumbria'.

This wonderfully evocative poem, one of the very earliest in the English language, was composed in the south but it speaks of the attitudes of both the Angles and the Saxons to Rome's architectural heritage:

Splendid this rampart is, though fate destroyed it,
The city buildings fell apart, the works
Of giants crumble. Tumbled are the towers,
Ruined the roofs, and broken the barred gate,
Frost in the plaster, all the ceilings gape,
Torn and collapsed and eaten up by age.

The Roman road through Craik Forest, still largely intact, still frequently travelled, passed close to the Anglian village of Hawick. It led to the ruined fort at Trimontium, Newstead, near Melrose. The Teviot Valley lay between two of the most massive defensive structures Europe has ever seen – the Antonine Wall to the north and, over the Cheviots, Hadrian's Wall. Born in its shadow, near modern Newcastle at a place called *Ad Murum*, 'at the Wall', Bede noted that it still stood 12 feet high and was 8 feet in breadth. A huge structure, it was an awesome testament to the power of imperial Rome and its greatest creation – a professional army.

Latin was not only the language spoken by the empire and its soldiers, it was also how priests spoke to God. The Christian church was adopted by pagan Northumbrian kings – the worshippers of Odin, Thor and Tiw – expressly to increase the sense of identity with Rome. Relatively close to Hawick and at the western terminal of the Wall was the very early Christian community of the Roman city of Carlisle. Probably the birthplace of both St Patrick and St Ninian, it had preserved within its walls much that was seen as civilised, much that harked back to the grandeur of the recent past. In 685, St Cuthbert, the Bishop of Lindisfarne, visited what was by then a Northumbrian possession and Wagga, the royal reeve of the city, showed him a working fountain, proof that the Roman water supply, with its pipes and aqueduct intact, was still working. A wall defended Carlisle so its grid of paved streets survived and, as late as the 12th century, the historian William of Malmesbury noted a large vaulted stone building. This may have been the Roman basilica or market hall and it carried an inscription to Mars and Venus.

To Saegifa and Rosfritha and their neighbours in 7th-century Hawick, the long shadow of Rome still fell on their humble houses even if they had never seen the Wall or what they called *enta geweorc*, 'the work of giants'. In church, they heard their priest pray in Latin and, through the stories of Christ, Pontius Pilate and the wanderings of the Apostles, they understood the ancient power of the empire.

Selkirk has perhaps a little more to say about Anglian Hawick. The name combines two Anglian words *sele* and *circe* and means 'the church by the hall'. In the Borders of 7th and 8th centuries, it seems that one often went with the other. One of the most complete and undisturbed Anglian settlements has been detected by aerial photography near Sprouston on the Tweed, east of Kelso. There, the clear outlines of a hall, a chapel and a graveyard can be made out. Sprouston is also the site of prehistoric earthworks and a remarkable wooden building probably dating to c. 3,000 BC. The potential similarities with early Hawick are striking.

If there was indeed an Anglian church on the mound of St Mary's, then there was almost certainly a hall nearby. Magically described in the poem *Beowulf*, early Anglian halls were built from planked timber in a rectangular layout. Secured in long foundation trenches, the plank walling was load bearing and buttressed at either gable. In all of the halls found in Southern Scotland – at Doon Hall and Whitekirk in East Lothian, Sprouston and just over the border at Yeavering – the doors were let into the long walls and, no doubt, all was decorated with carvings and with colour.

These buildings were central to the life of a community, the places where lords and their warbands feasted, where fires roared as ale and mead were drunk and where bards sang of glory. Perhaps the Hut at Hawick Common Riding is the lineal descendant of the hall at Anglian Hawick. Business was also done there, taxes paid, disputes settled and laws promulgated. In essence it was where a lord and his warriors lived, ate and slept. Here is Seamus Heaney's superb translation of *Beowulf*, where Hrothgar, King of the Shieldings, commands a hall to be built:

So his mind turned
To hall-building: he handed down orders
For men to work on a great mead-hall
Meant to be a wonder of the world forever;
It would be his throne-room and there he would dispense
His God-given goods to young and old –
But not the common land or people's lives.
Far and wide through the world, I have heard,
Orders for work to adorn that wallstead
Were sent to many peoples. And soon it stood there,
Finished and ready, in full view,
The hall of halls. Heorot was the name
He had settled on it, whose utterance was law.
Nor did he renege, but doled out rings
And torques at the table. The hall towered,
Its gables wide and high . . .

Beowulf beautifully describes the war culture of the Angles. Warbands were the fount of power and, when plunder flowed, more warriors joined and their lords waxed yet more powerful. Portable wealth such as gold, silver and precious stones were the lubricant – what warriors expected as a reward for loyalty and bravery in war. Always important, outward show marked out men. The more gold and silver a warrior wore, the greater he was – how else had he acquired such wealth if not through swordplay and steadfastness in the shield walls of many battles? The rings, torcs and precious metals doled out by kings and lords were the forerunners of medals. The shield wall, the manner in which battles were fought in the centuries before cavalry and archery began to take precedence, is the forerunner of a central tradition of the common ridings.

When captains called for the shield wall to form before battle, warriors closed up so that the rim of each shield was overlapping that of the man next to him. 'Rim to boss' was the call, so that a wall looked like the protective scales of a great fish. Most men are right-handed and when shield walls clashed and hand-to-hand fighting began, they swung and stabbed and exposed their right sides. That was why a right-hand man was so important. He could cover the exposed side of the man to his left, and the man to his right would cover him. A left-hand man was also important but less so.

Life for those who were not warriors – those who lived outside the hall – was very different. It is likely that Saegifa and Rosfritha were highborn women able and permitted to travel even the short distance to Cogsmill to worship at the Chapel of St Cuthbert. Or perhaps they had heard him preach there before any building was made. Others whose names have not come down to us lived much more humble lives. Houses were built of wooden frames and sods with thatched roofs. There were no windows and the only light came through a door. Heat for warmth and cooking came from a down-hearth, an arrangement of flat stones with a kerb around them set in the middle of a beaten earth floor. Smoke seeped through the thatch rather than a hole that would let in the weather. Since the hearth supplied the only light, most daily chores were done outside if the weather was warm and fair. House building had changed little from prehistoric times.

Archaeologists have discovered a characteristic Anglian building known as a *Grubenhaus* – literally, 'a sunken house'. Commonly, they were small rectangular structures around six metres by four metres with a floor half a metre deep. Probably workshops, several have been excavated and from the *Grubenhaus* found at Ratho, near Edinburgh, clay loom weights, spindle whorls and other gear associated with weaving have been recovered. If these buildings existed in Anglian Hawick – and it is likely that they did – then they speak of a very long tradition of textile production.

For much of the 7th century, the reach of Northumbrian kings seemed to extend again and again. Not only had they made themselves *Bretwaldas* in the south, they took over East Lothian as well as the Borders. Fife and West Lothian fell to them but, in 685, their apparently inexorable success came to a juddering halt. King Ecgfrith over-reached himself. At a pivotal battle at Dunnichen, near Forfar, the conquering Anglian army was scattered by a Pictish host led by King Bridei. Ecgfrith was killed and Anglian power shrank back to the shores of the Forth.

Nevertheless, the Northumbrian kings continued to consolidate their hold on Tweeddale and Teviotdale. In fact, it seems that the Borders became a power base – somewhere that an army could be raised. Northumbria had been formed from the union of two kingdoms – Bernicia and Deira. Bernicia included the Borders, Northumberland and part of Durham while Deira comprised most of Yorkshire. In 759, Aethelwald Moll seized the Northumbrian throne after the murder of Oswulf, the son and heir of King Eadberht. A Deiran nobleman, he attempted to assert himself in Bernicia. Here is the chronicler, Symeon of Durham:

> In the year 759 Aethelwald who was also called Moll, began to reign on the Nones [5th] of August.
>
> And in the beginning of his third year, a very severe battle was fought near Eildon on the eighth before the Ides [so on the 5th or 7th] of August; and in it Oswin fell, after three days, on the first day of the week. And King Aethelwald, who was called Moll, gained the victory in the battle.

Three days sounds more like a siege than a battle and rather than the prehistoric fort on the summit of Eildon Hill North, it is much more likely that Aethelwald Moll killed King Oswin of Northumbria at Trimontium, the old Roman fort at the foot of the hills.

In the second half of the 8th century, Offa of Mercia replaced the Northumbrian kings as the most powerful man in England and internal squabbling further weakened the once-glittering realm of the north but much worse than internecine struggles was about to burst over Britain. Sixty miles to the east of Hawick, more portents flashed in the sky – but these were not a prelude to the appearance of the sort of angelic hosts seen by Cuthbert. These were hosts of an entirely different kind. For the year 793, the *Anglo-Saxon Chronicle* reported:

> In that year terrible portents appeared in Northumbria and miserably afflicted the inhabitants; these were exceptional flashes of lightning and fiery dragons were seen flying in the air, and soon after in the same year the harrying of the heathen miserably destroyed God's church in Lindisfarne by rapine and slaughter.

Racing across twelve centuries, the shock of the first Viking attacks is palpable. Sailing out of the mists of the North Sea, out of nowhere, these ferocious, pagan warriors mounted surprise assaults on coastal monasteries and communities and killed, stole, tortured, raped and burned their way on to the pages of history. Irish chroniclers called them 'The Sons of Death'.

Hawick lay too far inland to be threatened by sea raiders but, once the Vikings began to settle in Britain, it seems that they came very close. Hogback tombstones mark the graves of wealthy Norse lords. They are carved as miniature houses of the dead with a curved roof beam (hence hogback) and small stone shingles are chiselled out on either side. Very distinctive, a massive example, two metres in length, can be found in Ancrum kirkyard and another, in Nisbet kirkyard, is almost as long. Both have neat rows of shingles carved on them. Two much smaller hogbacks have also been found at Lempitlaw near Kelso. And finally at Bedrule, three miles east of Hawick, two fragments of different stones lie near the church.

Hogback tombstones date to the 10th and 11th centuries and this cluster in Teviotdale shows that Norse lords wealthy enough to have them made controlled land in the Borders. No characteristic place names attest their presence but a peculiar echo of their pagan beliefs may have survived at the centre of Hawick's hallowed traditions.

Teribus Ye Teri Odin is a mysterious phrase. No one knows what it means or even what language the words come from. Thought to have been roared as a war cry, it has been adopted as Hawick's motto and the town's sons and daughters are known the world over as Teris. Sometimes their place of birth is called Teridom. No one is at all sure why.

More than a suspiciously convenient rhyme for Flodden, the last word 'Odin' supplies the only clue. If it is indeed an invocation of the Norse war god, Odin or Woden, then that suggests a link, a very tenuous link, with the men who lie under the hogback tombstones at Bedrule, Ancrum and Nisbet. Perhaps there was once an impressive tomb in Hawick, now lost.

However, all that may be, the older version of the phrase offers little help. *Tyr Haebbe Us, Ye Tyr Ye Odin* sounds like Old English, a later version of the language spoken by the Angles, but it makes no sense. Even though Hawick Common Riding is the time when *Teribus* is most sung and uttered, the war cry was not used – or, at least, recorded – before the 18th century. When James Hogg wrote the famous common riding song in 1819, the phrase was clearly seen as central, if enigmatic, even if its use was not ancient. All that can safely be said is that *Teribus* appears to be a long and unlikely connection with the Norse lords of Teviotdale in the 9th and 10th centuries.

Pressure from both the north and south began to compress the old kingdom of Northumbria. By the 10th century, the Wessex kings had grown powerful and Athelstan reduced Northumbrian kings to the rank of Earls of Bamburgh. And, at the same time, the ambitious Gaelic-speaking kings of Alba, of Scotland north of the Forth, looked to extend their reach over the Lothians and the Tweed and Teviot valleys. In the summer of 1018, Malcolm II MacAlpin led his host south to the narrow valley of the Caddon Water, between Galashiels and Selkirk. There he met his ally, King Owain of Strathclyde. As their men bivouacked by the burn, watering their horses, lighting cooking fires and sharpening their blades, the kings and their captains held a council of war. Scouts had told them that Eadulf, Earl of Bamburgh, had reached the Tweed with an army of spearmen, and this news persuaded Malcolm and Owain to hurry downriver to confront the Northumbrians before reinforcements could arrive.

They clashed at Carham, a sleepy hamlet now just inside the English border, probably on the flat haughland by a ford in the river. Blood soaked the grass as defeat turned into carnage. The Scottish host hacked the Anglian shield wall to pieces. Describing the aftermath of the battle in these terms, '[A]ll the people who dwelt between Tees and Tweed were well-nigh exterminated', the chronicler, Symeon of Durham was undoubtedly exaggerating but his doom-laden words sounded the death knell of Northumbrian power beyond the great river. 1018 was the probably the moment when Hawick found itself in the realm of Scottish kings, part of Scotland.

4

THE COMING OF THE WOLVES

FOUL-TEMPERED and wilful, much given to acts of unthinking violence, Ascelin, the Lord of Breherval in Brittany, became known as the Young Wolf. It was said that, when rebuffed as an unsuitable suitor for the hand of Isabel, the daughter of William de Breteuil, Ascelin's savage nature broke all the rules. Despite the fact that William was his lord and superior, the Young Wolf took him prisoner and tortured him until he agreed to give up his daughter in marriage as well as supply a substantial dowry. Legend embroiders the episode. Apparently, Ascelin had William stripped and tied him to a grating at the top of a tower in his castle. This took place in the depths of a bitter winter and in the biting cold winds and water was poured over the prisoner until ice began to form. At that point, William agreed that Isabel could marry Ascelin de Breherval and that he would receive a large dowry in gold.

However unlikely a tale, what emerges is the image of a man and a family of famous ill nature, ruthless in pursuit of gain – like many Normans. One historian has characterised the Norman expansion over Europe as 'Men With Beards Behaving Badly'. Young Wolf translates as Lupellus which, in turn, became the Norman surname of Lovell or Lovel. Ascelin's father, Robert de Breherval, sailed in the summer of 1066 with the invasion force of William the Bastard, Duke of Normandy. His victory at Hastings and the consequent subjugation of England delivered immense riches into the hands of all those who charged King Harold's shield wall on Senlac Hill. Ascelin became Lord of Castle Cary in Somerset some time after 1070. And, when his family took possession of this fertile territory and its little village, they did something that was repeated more than a thousand times all over England, Wales and Scotland.

Overlooking Castle Cary, two grassy mounds can now be seen – one much higher than the other. They were made by men directed by the Lovels. On a spur of higher ground, they had a motte-and-bailey castle built. These were simple structures and, in the ships of the invasion fleet, William the Conqueror had brought three that had been prefabricated in Normandy. Consisting of a simple mound – usually shaped like a huge Christmas pudding turned out on a plate (*motte* is the Norman-French word for 'a clod of earth'), with a wooden blockhouse on top – and a bailey – a palisaded courtyard – these castles could be thrown up in a matter of weeks. They acted as strongpoints, places of storage and, glowering over the village of Castle Cary, what archaeologists call 'a statement in the landscape'.

David MacMalcolm was immensely impressed with all things Norman. It seemed to him as though they understood the future and were ruthless enough to control it. Born in 1084, the sixth son of Malcolm II Canmore and his saintly Saxon Queen Margaret, David had few prospects. And these diminished to nearly nothing when his father and elder brother, Edward, were both killed on the same day in 1093 while raiding in Northumbria. Royal succession by primogeniture was a southern habit not yet accepted in Celtic Scotland and the Scottish earls installed the dead king's brother, Donald III Ban. He 'drove out the English who were with King Malcolm before'. Amongst the refugees fleeing south was the nine-year-old David MacMalcolm. With his older sister, Maud or Matilda, they sought sanctuary at the court of William II Rufus, the son of the Conqueror.

Events and accidents began to conspire in David's favour. In 1100, William Rufus was killed by a stray arrow while out hunting in the New

Forest. His heir, Robert Curthose, happened to be absent on crusade and his younger brother, Henry, seized the throne. To consolidate his position quickly, the usurper married Matilda, David's older sister. Their brother, Edgar, had recently succeeded in deposing Donald Ban and, no doubt, Henry thought that a dynastic union with Scotland would bolster his opportunism. It was a marriage that transformed David's world.

During his seven years at the Norman court, he had become known as David fitzMalcolm, the French patronymic prefix replacing the Gaelic. In Henry I's war against Robert Curthose, the young Scottish knight probably fought in the king's army. He will certainly have learned to speak Norman-French fluently – and almost certainly come into contact with Ascelin de Breherval of Castle Cary and his three sons. After the defeat of Curthose at Tinchebrai in Normandy in 1106, those loyal to Henry regained their French possessions and David was granted land in the Cotentin – the Cherbourg Peninsula. It was an area that would produce many names famous in Scottish history – the Bruces and the Stewarts amongst them.

Chance worked once more in David's favour. In 1107, King Edgar of Scotland died and was succeeded by Alexander I. But Edgar had been generous and bequeathed David a huge tract of Southern Scotland, Galloway, bits of Cumbria, Tweeddale and Teviotdale. Understandably, Alexander I objected but Earl David's brother-in-law was persuasive. Henry I made it clear that an Anglo-Norman army would march north in support of the young man's inheritance. And, as further protection, the Earl David brought Norman lords and their soldiers with him to establish control of the south. Amongst them was a son of Ascelin, the Young Wolf – a Lovel.

Hawick was clearly seen as a lordship – a territory with both a legal identity and a considerable value. It had been the home of Saegifa and Rosfritha as early as the 7th century and, as the presence of drengs and boon workers attests, it may have been a pendicle to the royal shire of Jedburgh or perhaps the property of the Bishop of Durham. By the time of King Edgar, it had become a royal possession – a place he could bequeath to his brother, David. And it was enough of a temptation to bring the Lovels and their armed retinue north to the kingdom of Scotland in support of the young man. David held the rank of earl but some documents talked of him as *comes* or Count David, in the Norman style, and there is even one reference to him as Princeps Cumbriae or Prince David of Cumbria. Whatever the nomenclature, his brother Edgar had made the young man immensely wealthy and powerful and he was determined to develop his inheritance in ways he had observed in England.

Roaring instructions in as much Early Scots as they could muster, while speaking to each other in Norman French, the Lovels' men began to build their motte and bailey above the village of Hawick. Without doubt, local men and women will have been pressed into service as labourers. As at Castle Cary, they had chosen ground higher than the village, a spur of land that runs out from Crumhaugh Hill, part of the watershed between Teviot and Slitrig. To the east, a steep bank provided a handy natural defensive feature and a convenient way down it will have been found so that the Slitrig could supply the motte with water. To build up the Christmas pudding-shaped mound, it is likely that a stout stake was first banged into the ground roughly at the centre of the preferred location. Then a rope was attached, pulled tight before men walked around describing a reasonably accurate circle. Once the perimeter of the motte had been marked out, the digging and mounding began.

In April 1912, Alexander O. Curle, a scion of the Melrose family of antiquarians, was granted permission by the town council to have trenches dug at the base of the motte. Believing there to have been a ditch around it, he opened three narrow trenches on three sides. Curle discovered that his conjecture was correct. A broad defensive ditch had been dug and it measured 28 feet across with a maximum depth of 7 feet. Pottery and a coin found at the bottom confirmed an early medieval date and later finds – part of a modern glass bottle and the head of a clay pipe – showed that it had been filled in much more recently, perhaps the middle of the 19th century. The ditch may have been planted with thorns or quickset – something the Lovels could not have known was very appropriate to Hawick.

Curle also measured the motte accurately, noting that it rose to a maximum height of 28 feet 7 inches, and he reckoned that it had been constructed on a level platform cut into the sloping site. Mattocks, wooden shovels and wicker baskets probably comprised the workers' toolkit and it will have been backbreaking labour with Lovel's men encouraging speed. They will have wanted their new motte to rise quickly so that they could build a wooden blockhouse on its summit – somewhere safe, dry and dominating.

Any remnant of the bailey appears to have been completely obliterated. It lay to the north-east of the motte but its size can only be estimated. A ditch will also have been dug around its perimeter and, on the upcast, a palisade of sharpened stakes will have been rammed in – *palus* is the Latin word for 'a stake'. It gave rise to the phrase 'beyond the pale' for those who lived outside a protected perimeter, meaning something like savages – in this case, the people of Hawick. While Lord Lovel and his family first lived in the relative security of the blockhouse on the motte, his retainers occupied the bailey. Stables and storerooms were also built and a fortified gateway was constructed, probably at the north-easternmost end of the palisade.

These elementary castles were most vulnerable to fire or a protracted siege. The stakes and the ditch discouraged a frontal assault and the steep sides of the motte made any kind of attack by cavalry impossible. As the Normans secured their conquest, these structures were quickly raised in towns such as Lincoln, Norwich and Cambridge. There, houses were summarily destroyed to clear an open space and create a distance between the sort of cover buildings could provide for attackers who wanted to approach unseen and surprise the palisade and the bailey. Windsor Castle is the most famous surviving motte-and-bailey castle, with the Christmas pudding-shaped mound clearly visible. This need for open ground around the fortifications was another reason why the Hawick Mote was some distance from the medieval village. St Mary's, on its own mound, was probably the closest substantial building.

Once established, the Lovels governed from their little castle. It may have been eventually converted into stone buildings but no trace remains. Courts will have been held there and harsh medieval justice dispensed. As late as 1484, the Baron of Hawick granted charters 'at the principal messuage [building] of the barony of Hawick, called the Mote'. Even though a stone tower had been built in the town by that time, the Mote appeared to retain some sort of legal status.

In the centuries following the Norman Conquest, the new masters of the countryside maintained a clear cultural divide between themselves and the natives. It was not until the end of the 14th century that an English king, Richard II, spoke English. And, following his upbringing at the Anglo-Norman court of Henry I, David I almost certainly conducted business in French, although his charters were often self-consciously cosmopolitan. In his confirmation of the lands of Selkirk Abbey (soon to move downriver to Kelso) in 1120, his clerks wrote, 'David the Earl, son of Malcolm King of Scots, [gives] greetings to all of his friends, French, English and Scots, all of whom are sons of the Holy Church of God.' And, at the end of the document:

> These are the witnesses; the aforementioned Bishop John [of Glasgow], Countess Matilda, Henry son of the Earl, Walter the Chaplain, Osbert the Chaplain, Alwyn the Chaplain, William nephew of the Earl, Robert de Bruis, Robert de Umfraville, Walter de Bolebec, Robert de Painton, Cospatric brother of Dalphin, Hugh de Moreville, Pagano de Braiosa, Robert Corbet, Reginald de Muscamp, Walter de Lindsey, Robert de Burneville, Cospatric the Sheriff, Cospatric son of Aldeve, Uchtred son of Scot, Macchus, Colbanus, Gillemichael, Odardo Sheriff of Bamburgh, Lyulf son of Uchtred, Radulph the Englishman, Aimar the Gallovidian, Roger de Leicester, Adam the Chamberlain.

At least half of these men are identifiably Norman, and when Earl David became king in 1124 more and more new people were given lands in the Borders, including the Lovels. Perhaps the most striking innovation was the founding of the four Border abbeys, all of them the creation of orders of reformed monks either directly or originally from France. Almost every one of these incoming families retained links with the south and the Lovels of Hawick were no exception. Documents relating to the archbishopric of St Andrews reveal some detail. In the 1150s, Henry Lovel granted to the canons at St Andrews land at Branxholme, which must have been part of the estate given by David I. Henry's son, Richard, then changed these arrangements and swapped the land at Branxholme for land in the barony of Hawick. This was confirmed by Pope Lucius III in 1183. Henry Lovel's status as a major magnate was underlined by the appearance of his name as a witness to a royal charter of 1166 conveying to Robert Bruis, another Norman whose family would later become royal, his lands in Annandale.

Scotland prospered in the 12th and 13th centuries. In what seems to have been a long period of higher temperatures and extended growing seasons, the medieval climatic optimum, more land was brought into cultivation. The population almost certainly rose. Under the guidance of the entrepreneurial hands of the astute Border abbots, sheep farming was undertaken on a near-industrial scale. Textile production in Flanders and Italy had intensified as an organised network of outworkers became common and demand for wool for their looms rose. Sheep ranches in the Lammermuirs ('the Lambs' Moors'), the Cheviots and the hill country south-west of Hawick expanded and the spring clip was sold to Flemish and Italian merchants at the markets at Roxburgh, near Kelso. Now completely effaced, it was the earliest urban centre in Scotland and woolpacks sold there were taken down the Tweed to be loaded on to ships at the busy Berwick quays.

Sources are sparse for the medieval history of Hawick but the Lovels appear to have flourished. They certainly argued a great deal amongst themselves over their possessions and their disputes shed a fractious light on continuing links with Somerset and Castle Cary. In 1207, Lady Matilda Lovel brought an action in the south against her brother-in-law, Henry Lovel. She claimed that her late husband, Ralph Lovel, had controlled the family possessions in Hawick and that, therefore, on his death, she was entitled to all or part of them. The English records are unclear. Henry settled the dispute by gifting Matilda the manor of Hunewic in Somerset as well as handing over 16 oxen (four plough teams) and 23 merks in silver. This sounds substantial and Matilda must have had a good case. The sense of Castle Cary and Hawick being held together as a family's lordship, perhaps even as a single legal entity so far as ownership and rights were concerned, is reinforced in 1248 when yet another argument erupted between the warring Lovels. This time, Christina Lovel, probably the widow of Henry Lovel, brought a case against his brother, Richard. Prompted by her second husband, she maintained that she had the right to nominate the priest at the church at Cavers. No record of the verdict survives but, given the persistence of feisty Lovel women, the odds must be that her action succeeded. And her determination begins a tradition as early as the 13th century of feisty women in Hawick.

With Branxholme and the barony of Hawick (which may have been an inclusive term – but its early extent is not recorded), Cavers appears to have formed part of the Lovels' Scottish holdings. Even now, the Ordnance Survey shows a detailed, old landscape showing many traces and phases of occupation. Cavers Kirk first comes on record in 1116 as part of the bishopric of Glasgow (which had successfully claimed Teviotdale from Durham by the 12th century) but the unused and impressive building by the roadside was probably not on the site of the original. Close to Cavers House are the remains of an older church and hard by its site is the socket of an old preaching cross. In the absence of church buildings in the early centuries of Christianity, priests would summon the faithful with a handbell to gather around a cross. Like the wonderful examples at Bewcastle and Ruthwell, these often had biblical scenes carved on the faces of the shaft and crosspieces and were painted in vivid colours. The old cross at Cavers speaks of antiquity – perhaps an Anglian foundation that was known to Saegifa and Rosfritha. By the early Middle Ages, when the Lovels were bickering about who had the right to appoint the priest, Cavers parish was vast – it stretched west into Upper Teviotdale, as far as Mosspaul, and it also included the village of Denholm – and produced a substantial income.

The Lovels appear to have insinuated themselves into royal favour and they began to attend the court. Alexander III may have knighted Sir Robert Lovel. He was certainly of sufficient status to act as a negotiator with the Norwegians in the business of contracting a marriage between the king's daughter and Eric, King of Norway. In her turn, their daughter, the Maid of Norway, would become fleetingly important to the history of Scotland after 1286.

Robert Lovel held Hawick, Branxholme and Cavers in feudal tenure as a subject of the Scottish king. This involved a simple but vital exchange. In return for loyalty, the provision of an agreed number of soldiers to serve in the royal host and certain obligations of hospitality, the Lovels became hereditary lords of what may have been a considerable part of south-west Roxburghshire.

But they were not only subjects of Alexander III. In 1263, Richard Lovel did homage to Henry III of England when he inherited his father's lands in Somerset. And, of course, there was an argument. Richard's brother, Hugh, contested the inheritance of his sisters, Christina and Alicia, at Castle Cary. This set of dual feudal obligations in two kingdoms was by no means unusual in medieval Scotland amongst Anglo-Norman families who had originally come from the south. David I was also Earl of Northampton and Huntingdon and he did homage to the English king for these valuable and extensive lands and the Bruces also held English lordships. But, in the case of the Lovels, this divided loyalty was to prove determinant.

In the summer of 1214, Hawick celebrated. A procession of

notables led by Adam, Bishop of Caithness, recently Abbot of Melrose, made its way through the village to dedicate the parish church to the Virgin Mary. In the Borders, there appears to have been something of a cult around St Mary since all four of the great abbeys at Kelso, Melrose, Jedburgh and Dryburgh were also dedicated to the Mother of Christ. As the Lord Bishop and his followers moved towards the church, psalms were sung and a censer swung incense in their path. Almost certainly through the patronage of the Lovels, the Lords of Hawick, the old church appears to have been rebuilt and some decorated stonework has survived from the medieval period. The occasion will have been made festive for local people with food and ale in the kirkyard and, if the sun shone, it will have glinted off the lavish cope and staff of the bishop and the Lovels and others in their aristocratic finery.

Christian belief was enormously powerful and was also thought to pay posthumous dividends. If the Lovels could have negotiated directly with God, they would have. Instead, they will have expected to spend considerably less time in the celestial waiting room known as purgatory and perhaps even avoid damnation altogether in return for bearing the cost of rebuilding St Mary's. And they will probably have reserved the right to be buried close to the church's altar. The concept of holy ground was, to them, not abstract but very real and under the floor of a church of some antiquity, where St Cuthbert may have walked and that had also been blessed and consecrated by a bishop, was a good place for a sinful baron of Hawick to be planted. In the Middle Ages, it was a firmly held belief that that holy soil had the power to cleanse the corpse of sin. The rotting away of the sinful flesh after burial was the outward sign of this process. At Bishop Adam's monastery of Melrose, these articles of faith were actively encouraged as a source of income. Ailing and aged aristocrats gave land, possessions and money to become novice monks before they died so that they were guaranteed burial inside the sacred precincts, in the ground where saints had trod. It was called taking holy orders *ad succurrundum*, 'done in a hurry'. It is likely that the Lovels were in more of a hurry than most.

The night of 19 March 1286 was stormy. Strong winds whipped up the spindrift off the Firth of Forth, rain spattered the royal feasting hall at Edinburgh Castle. But King Alexander III of Scotland was unabashed, he was celebrating his marriage to the beautiful Yolande de Dreux and, perhaps flushed with wine, he was determined to share her bed – that very night. The problem was that his new bride was at the royal manor at Kinghorn, across the storm-tossed Forth. Despite entreaties from his anxious courtiers, Alexander called for his horse to be saddled, rode to South Queensferry and crossed safely. Perhaps all would be well. But, somewhere along the cliff path to Kinghorn, the king became detached from his retinue and his horse probably lost its footing in the wind and the dark. The following morning, search parties found Alexander III's body on the beach, at the foot of a steep and rocky slope. His neck was broken. Scotland was immediately plunged into a dynastic crisis. All three of the king's children had died and the heir presumptive was Margaret, the Maid of Norway, his granddaughter. She died before she reached Scotland. Alexander's rashness was to cost his realm dear. After the wind and rain of 19 March 1286, much greater storms burst over Scotland as the kingdom without a king began the nightmare of the Wars of Independence.

Fought nearly thirty years after Alexander's death, Bannockburn was emphatic. Over two days in late June 1314, Robert the Bruce and his captains' skill at manoeuvring the huge English army into a position that would even up the numerical odds and produce an unlikely victory was decisive and it brought a temporary end to the tremendously destructive war with England. Armies had crossed and recrossed the Borders leaving trails of destruction and despoliation. Hawick, however, may have avoided the worst effects of the war, certainly at the hands of the dominant and larger English armies and raiding parties. The Lovels remained loyal to Edward I and Edward II of England and not only was their barony off the track usually beaten by armies marching north (they used the old Roman roads of Dere Street to traverse the Cheviots or came via Berwick or waded across the Solway fords), it was also a parcel of land held by a family who backed the Plantagenet claim to the overlordship of Scotland.

In the years before Bannockburn and Bruce's guerrilla war against the English, the king of Scots gained control of much of Teviotdale while the enemy held the fertile fields of the lower Tweed and the mighty castle of Roxburgh. The Lovels were expelled from Branxholme and Hawick and Bruce granted their lands to Sir Henry Baliol. In return for loyalty in a largely hostile land, the dispossessed Lovels were given Old Roxburgh by the English king. They did not hold it for long.

Standing on a partly manmade oblong mound very close to the banks of the Teviot and about half a mile from the Tweed on the other side, close to where the rivers join at Kelso, Roxburgh Castle was very formidable. Behind its massive walls were several great towers, the church of St John and accommodation for hundreds of defenders. Like some of the larger mottes, it was probably accessible from the town of Roxburgh by a wooden bridge at its eastern end and, to the west, substantial remains of gateposts can still be seen at the only point where the castle mound is not impossibly steep. It was protected by a moat, fed by a weir on the Teviot. But, in 1314, Roxburgh was taken in a daring assault by the Scots.

Reputedly on Fastern's E'en, the old name for the last Tuesday before Lent, now known by older people as Shrove Tuesday, when the garrison was feasting at a carnival, in the original sense of the word, the Scots stole into the mighty castle. Carnival literally means 'farewell to meat' and, before the fasting and deprivations imposed by the church during the period of Lent, it was a common habit to hold a banquet where meat was served in abundance. Led by Sir James Douglas, known to history as The Black Douglas, a force of Scots approached the walls of Roxburgh on a moonless night before scaling them and overpowering the lookouts. In his epic *The Brus*, the bard John Barbour added colour when he sang that the Black Douglas's men had covered themselves in their cloaks and crept on all fours so that they resembled cattle. Maybe. In any event, the garrison of impregnable Roxburgh was forced to surrender. Perhaps Sir Richard Lovel was amongst them.

Later that year, in the blood-soaked ruck of battle at Bannockburn, many English knights were killed as the Scottish schiltrons charged and drove them back into their own ranks to be crushed and stabbed to death in a fatal scrummage. Amongst the bodies identified later was that of Sir John Lovel, the second baron of Castle Cary. King Robert the Bruce was ruthless in punishing those who had opposed him and unhesitating in rewarding his supporters with the forfeited lands of their enemies. After Bannockburn, little more is heard of the Lovels of Hawick.

The aristocratic name that came to dominate the remainder of the medieval period belonged to the Douglases. Ambitious, violent, charismatic and lucky, they had built up such huge territories by the beginning of the 15th century that modern historians write of the Douglas Empire. In a Scotland where weak, absent or juvenile kings could be manipulated – even removed – they thrived as adroit power brokers. The Douglases' ownership of Hawick was only one of many possessions and by no means in the first rank of importance. It was probably first granted to Sir James Douglas, the hero of Roxburgh, after the 1330s. He certainly held Cavers and Liddesdale at that time.

After the death of Robert the Bruce from leprosy in 1329, Edward, the son of the deposed King John Baliol, led an army of the dispossessed into Scotland. They were magnates, like the Lovels, who had marched north to fight for the return of their forfeited lands. After initial success, Edward was forced to flee. Much of the 14th century saw warfare in the Borders and, when Jedburgh and its castle found itself in English hands, justice was administered at Hawick. Because they were the largest buildings available, churches were often used to hold court sessions and other secular meetings. As a reward for the recapture of Roxburgh Castle in 1342, Sir Alexander Ramsay had been appointed Sheriff of Teviotdale. As he presided at St Mary's, a disturbance was heard outside the main door and riding up through the kirkyard was Sir William Douglas with a band of armed men at his back. The Hawick crowd parted as Douglas strode up the aisle with his sword drawn. He was furious that he had been passed over for the office of sheriff and determined to take the law into his own hands, so to speak. There followed a fierce swordfight in front of the altar until a bleeding and badly wounded Ramsay was bundled on to the back of a horse. Douglas and his men spurred their mounts up the Slitrig road with their prisoner. For seventeen days Ramsay rotted in a black-dark dungeon under Hermitage Castle without food or water. It was later said that he survived for so long because there was a granary on the floor above and grains dropped through the cracks, enough to keep him alive a little longer. On Ramsay's miserable death from starvation and dehydration, Sir William Douglas was briskly appointed Governor of Roxburgh Castle and Sheriff of Teviotdale. Such was the exercise of justice and politics in the 14th-century Border country.

Douglas's brutality chimed with the harshness of the climate. Since Bannockburn, it had been changing quickly. Flushed with victory, King Robert led an invasion of England and, in the spring of 1315, laid siege to the old Roman city of Carlisle and its dour castle. Heroic resistance was directed by Sir Andrew de Harcla, a local lord who was created Earl of Carlisle for his efforts. But the more compelling reason for the city's survival was not dogged defence – it was rain. In the spring of 1315, unusually heavy and persistent rain fell all over Europe and, around Carlisle's stout walls, Bruce's siege engines became bogged down and were easily toppled in the soaking ground, his army encampment was washed out and little food could be commandeered locally. It was the beginning of the Little Ice Age – a series of periods of bad and cold weather that was to grip Europe for more than five hundred years. The rain not only drove Bruce from Carlisle in 1315, it continued into 1316 and there was widespread famine across Europe. Crops failed, bread was hugely expensive, no winter forage could be cut and herds and flocks had to be slaughtered. By the summer of 1317 the rain relented but hunger had depleted and weakened the population. In Scotland between 10–25 per cent died and food production did not return to normal until the mid 1320s. Medieval governments simply could not deal with the crisis caused by climate change, and famine and criminal activity became common as people were forced to steal to live. But it was religious faith that may have been rocked most severely. Prayer and intercession had no effect and the 14th century saw the rise of new beliefs across Europe, in what were immediately cast as heretical sects.

This dramatic change in the climate of Northern Europe ended a period of 200 years of expansion. Between 1100 and 1300, the population of Scotland may have doubled to reach one million. Before the onset of the Little Ice Age, the number of people living in Roxburghshire has been credibly estimated at 27,000, 2.7 per cent of all Scots. About 90 per cent of that number lived and worked on the land and the average density per square mile was about 35, perhaps rising to 50 on the better land of the middle Tweed. That meant only 10 per cent of the people of Roxburghshire lived in towns and villages. Most will have been concentrated in Roxburgh itself and Kelso, Jedburgh and Melrose, where the great abbeys had settlements beyond the precinct walls. That probably means a population for Hawick in 1300 of no more than 200 or so – 30 or 40 houses at most clustering around the Church of St Mary at the confluence of the Slitrig and the Teviot.

The 14th century was a time of tremendous turmoil, especially in the Borders. Not only did the soggy depredations of the Little Ice Age deplete the population, the English returned in force in the 1340s and much of the best land lay in their hands for another forty years. Edward III was a powerful warlord and, even though his prime military objective was the recovery of English possessions in France, he kept a tight grip on southern Scotland. In this, he was helped by the weakness of Scottish kingship and by another, far more destructive, demographic disaster.

At Caddonfoot near Galashiels, a Scottish army gathered for a retaliatory raid into England. Their captains saw what they called 'the foul death of the English' – the devastating arrival of the Black Death in the summer of 1348 – as an opportunity. Believing that this English disease would not affect them, the army attacked Durham and, of course, brought the contagion back north as unwelcome booty. By 1350, it was raging through towns, villages and farm places. Originating in China, the Black Death swept west to Europe and spread quickly to England where it killed between 30–50 per cent of the inhabitants – between 3 and 5 million people. Those parameters may have been a little less disastrous in Scotland but not by much.

The plague was carried by fleas and infected human beings through contact with rats. Also known as bubonic plague, it attacked the lymph glands to cause swelling and then made its deadly way into the bloodstream. A variant was pneumonic plague and it was transmitted through the air rather than by touch. Death was rapid – only three or four days after the symptoms appeared. The consequences of such a pandemic were dramatic and long lasting. A shortage of farm labour drove up wages but caused output to decline, while the death of many priests through contact with their parishioners contributed to a slackening in the certainties of belief. But, in one way, the Black Death did benefit Scotland. In 1346, two years before its arrival in England, Edward III's army had defeated the Scots at the Battle of Neville's Cross near Durham and the young king seemed set to realise his grandfather's dream of subjugating Scotland. Disease diverted him and the danger of complete English domination passed. But, in the Borders, a continuing occupying presence did not improve the conditions of life for ordinary people as raids and counter-raids galloped across the landscape. In 1364, the Chamberlain at Berwick (a tax collector) reported to the London Exchequer that no rents could be raised in Hawick because of the devastation caused by the Scots.

This must have been disappointing for the Lovel family. Richard had successfully petitioned Edward III for the return of his lands at Hawick but it is not clear that he ever took possession of them. Branxholme was in the hands of an English lord who was simply described as 'Inglis'.

Reconquest eventually began to gather momentum and, by 1369, Scots magnates had retaken lands around Earlston and, by the 1370s, English territory had been whittled down to Roxburgh, its castle, the nearby suburb of Kelso and a narrow corridor between it and Jedburgh's well-set castle. It remained in enemy hands until 1408 when Sir William Douglas of Drumlanrig took it. Jedburgh's walls were tumbled down rather than risk it falling to the English once more. Only Roxburgh and Berwick remained occupied.

War was changing. In the 15th century, artillery began to play a much more significant role. Guns were probably cast at a foundry near Galashiels, perhaps even at the place now known as Gun Knowe. James II of Scotland was fascinated by their power and range. In 1460, he led an army to the foot of Roxburgh's castle walls and a huge cannon called The Lion was set up. Tradition holds that it was emplaced in a trench on the far side of the Tweed, below where Floors Castle stands now, out of range of the guns of Roxburgh but of a large enough calibre to reach the enemy walls from such a distance. A chronicler writing in early Scots recorded what happened next:

> King James hauing sik pleasure in discharging gret gunis past til a place far fra the armie to recreat himself in schuting gret pieces, quhairof he was verie expert, bot the piece appeiringlie, with ouer sair a charge, flies in flinderis, with a part of quhilk, strukne in the hench or he was war, quhairof (allace) he dies.

The cost of taking Roxburgh was great but its fall can be seen as the last act in the two hundred year War of Independence, much of it fought on Border soil. Once the castle was in Scots hands, like Jedburgh, its walls were 'doung to the ground'.

In 1452, the grant of the barony of Hawick to William Douglas of

Drumlanrig in Dumfriesshire was reconfirmed and, sixty years later, his successor and descendant began to develop his inheritance. Sir William Douglas enacted two legal documents which may be said to stand at the outset of the town's modern history. After a dispute with the royal court over the extent of his rights, he made Hawick into a free burgh of barony in 1511. This status may have been formalised at that time but there are hints that it was not new. Hawick burgesses appear in earlier records. In 1433, Simon Routledge is said to have been a burgess and he may indeed be the first named Hawick man in the story of the town. Aristocrats, bishops, priests and saints all appear before 1433 but Simon may be the first townsman to boast that Hawick was his home and not a possession or a place to preach.

More than 300 burghs of barony were given formal charters in Scotland between 1450 and 1707. Some were speculative and never amounted to anything. In the Borders, Rutherford, Linton and Smailholm remained as hamlets and villages while Longnewton, near St Boswells, has completely disappeared. Others prospered. Burghs were entitled to hold markets, usually weekly, and burgesses were free men who were allowed to trade in the town. They also enjoyed the right to graze their beasts and cut peats on the common. The dividend for kings and aristocrats was that burghs and their markets generated tax and toll revenue.

The provision of the vital resource of grazing and fuel gathering was the subject of Sir William's second legal measure. He granted to the new burgh a substantial parcel of land, much of it to the south. In a confirmation of the original charter of 1511 that was issued in 1537, it is described as 'le common hauch et le common mure de Hawick'. The language implies that everyone understood what was meant – a hint that the existence of the common predated 1511 and Douglas was only regularising what had been customary. Amounting to 1,549 acres, it was mostly upland, much of the watershed between the Slitrig and the Teviot. Here is an early description of the bounds of the common. The only eccentric spelling is *Fynnik* for 'Fenwick'. It lay '[b]etween Burnford on the east, Troutlawford on the west, and the syke of Wintownmoss on the south, and the dykes of Goldelands and Fynnik on the north sides from one to the other'.

In addition to grazing and fuel, the common also supplied roofing and flooring in the shape of heather and bracken. Firewood will also have been gathered at one time but, since this is a resource that quickly runs out, this must have been controlled. In an era before shops or supermarkets, all households grew, reared or gathered much of their food. A cow was essential and sheep relatively easy to keep for milk, meat and wool. Also vital to the people of Hawick was the ancient journey of transhumance – the moving of beasts up to the higher summer pastures. This was a vital moment in the rhythms of the agricultural year. As new spring grass forced its way through the yellow wrack of winter in the upland pastures, townspeople had to be able to move their beasts off and relieve garden and lowland plots in and close to Hawick. In April or May, depending on the weather, they drove their cows and sheep up to the common where they would thrive on the sweet new growth. It was open, unfenced pasture and some towns employed a common herdsman to keep a check on animals. Several burns run through the Hawick common and these supplied sufficient water. The real dangers were a wet summer and the boggy, undrained ground, particularly in the southern pastures.

Since it was essential that its broad acres could support all of the townspeople's beasts in the summer and autumn, it was very important that the common was protected. Neighbouring landowners often attempted to encroach and the detailed history of Selkirk's common in the 16th century tells of many such attempts. One dispute with the Kers of Greenhead ended with the murder of the Selkirk Provost, John Mithag and one of his bailies, James Keyne, as they rode to Edinburgh in the summer of 1541 to obtain confirmation of the town's legal rights.

The violent death of John Deans in 1546 may be associated with the protection of the Hawick common. An elaborate table gravestone was made and around the edge was carved 'Johne Deinis slan in debait of his nichtbouris geir, the zeir of God MDXLVI'. Sometimes used for stolen goods in the times of the reivers, *geir* or gear was a term for anything portable and, therefore, easily lifted. Deans' death may have taken place at Skelfhill and may have occurred on a common riding. That might explain the erection of such an elaborate memorial in St Mary's kirkyard – a local hero honoured.

As these instances suggest, common ridings began not as ceremonies but as necessary and occasionally violent annual checks on the bounds and burgesses were compelled to attend. Numbers of riders (or walkers) mattered if there was to be a confrontation with the retainers of a local lord. In 1640, the heavy penalties for burgesses who did not turn up on Common Riding Day (usually at the end of May) are set out: 'Whatsomever person that beis not present yeirlie at the common ryding and setting the faires, sal pay forty shillings, toties quoties, and wardit without license or ane lawful excuse.'

Two years after his grant of the common to Hawick, Sir William Douglas was dead, his body one of thousands that lay on Flodden's blood-soaked field.

International politics once again had baleful effects on the Borders. The boundless ambition of Henry VIII took his army to France and, when the town of Therouanne fell to him and he laid siege to Tournai, the French appealed to their Scottish allies. Desperately needing to distract the English and divide their forces, their queen implored James IV 'to advance a yard into England'. Sensing an opportunity after generations of suffering at the hands of English kings, he assembled a vast host on the Burgh Muir of Edinburgh, perhaps more than 20,000, one of the largest ever to rumble out of Scotland. One author has estimated the Scots army at an extraordinary 42,000. They began to move south on 21 August 1513.

Anxious to follow a thorough strategy, James IV planned to besiege the formidable castles of north Northumberland. Seventeen large bombards were wheeled south on bogeys to the banks of the

Tweed opposite Norham Castle. After six days of pounding with huge gunstones, the garrison surrendered. James went on to take the castles of Wark, Etal and Ford, establishing his headquarters at Ford.

Meanwhile, Henry VIII despatched an old warrior to raise an army in the north of England. Remembering ancient allegiances, the seventy-year-old Earl of Surrey stopped at Durham Cathedral to take the banner of St Cuthbert before going on to the muster at Alnwick. At that point, a curiously mannered exchange began. Couched in the elaborate and courtly language of chivalry, a message carried by the herald known as Rouge Croix Pursuivant arrived at the camp of James IV at Ford Castle. The Earl of Surrey wished to enquire if the Scottish king was prepared to do battle on the 9th of September at some time between 12 noon and 3 p.m. Perhaps he also asked if that would be convenient. A day later, after a suitable interval, the Islay Herald was sent to Surrey's camp with a polite message saying that the proposed arrangements would be suitable. Thank you. The substantial issue behind all of this flummery was logistical – how could two such huge bodies of men and animals stay in the field for long without running out of food? They had to join battle or disperse and, having undertaken a muster and all that it involved, neither Surrey nor James IV wished to withdraw.

On 5 September the Scots moved from Ford and took up a well-defended position with commanding views to the south and east, the directions from which the English would surely approach. Lookouts on Flodden Hill watched the English advance in three battalions protected by mounted flankers and scouts across the Milfield Plain. They camped at Barmoor and the Earl of Surrey composed another message for the Rouge Croix Pursuivant. He complained to the Scottish king that his well-chosen position was unchivalrous and that they should fight in open field. To his credit, James IV ignored this nonsense but Surrey had devised a surprise.

Scouts reported that the English battalions were moving north towards the Tweed. Were they planning to raid into Berwickshire?

Then they suddenly swung left and crossed the River Till at Twizel and Straw Ford. Surrey's plan became clear. He planned to position his army directly north of the Scots, between James's army and the Tweed, making any retreat very difficult.

The day was windy and it began to rain. Once Surrey reached Branxton, his gunners raked the Scottish ranks and were very destructive. By contrast, James IV's guns could not be trained low enough to fire downhill and their gunstones whistled over the heads of the English, their trajectory always too high. And then the Scots' gunnery master was killed, effectively silencing their artillery. In the wind and rain, archery was useless. James believed that he had no option but to advance downhill, giving up his dominant position, and attack.

The ground was very wet and, even though men cast off their shoes to find a better footing, the Scottish ranks began to break up as men charged at variable speeds. Also, they had real difficulty in controlling their huge, 17-foot pikes. At half the length and with axe, hook and spearheads, the English halberds suited the conditions much better since they could parry the cumbersome pikes and the front ranks of the Scots began to fall.

James IV had made a profound tactical error in choosing to charge downhill in the van of his battalion. As soon as they engaged with the front rank of the English, he became buried in the ruck of the fighting, unable to see what was happening more than a few yards in front of him, unable to direct his forces in any way. By contrast, Surrey led from the back, probably on a horse so that he could see the ebb and flow of the battle and make adjustments accordingly. On the Scottish left flank, a battalion of Borderers and Aberdeenshire men had driven back the English right but, on the right, the Highlanders had been routed. After some hours of desperate hand-to-hand fighting, the king's battalion in the centre was rolled up and a terrible slaughter began.

A king, nine earls, two abbots, fourteen great lords and many ordinary men such as ploughmen, weavers and burgesses died at Flodden as well as Sir William Douglas. But, given that Lord Home pulled his Borderers back from the left wing after Lord Dacre contained their early advance, it is likely that fewer ordinary Borderers died than is traditionally believed. But there was carnage nonetheless and the Borders would certainly suffer in the years to follow.

Some were watching and waiting. The riders known as the 'banditti' of Teviotdale and Tynedale went on to attack the deserted English camp, rifling tents and stealing horses. And they also shadowed the retreating remnant of the Scottish army, like vultures, hoping for stragglers to fall behind. These incidents were fell portents of what the 16th century would bring. The days of the Border Reivers were dawning.

5

THE LORDS OF THE NAMES

GEORDIE BURN knew the hill trails through the Cheviots well – their seasons and moods, which were passable in winter and those that offered cover and avoided the prying eyes of farm places or villages. Late September in 1596 was a good time of the year to lift cattle grown fat on the summer's grass but the nights were still light and some flocks and herds would still be out on the hills. And the sharp-eyed herd-laddies could see movement over the treeless moorland from a long way off. And it was best to avoid the old Roman road even though its metalled surface made for solid and dry going in all weathers. Geordie had only three men who had ridden over the border with him from the Jedforest – his uncle, Jock Burn, and two retainers. It was enough to keep a small herd of cattle together but too few to resist a resolute attack. Dere Street will have had groups of travellers, perhaps even some patrols of the March Warden's men, and it passed too close to Redesdale's bastle house inside the walls of the old fort at High Rochester. Better to follow the byways over the watershed hills. Perhaps Clennel Street, the old trail from Harbottle to the lovely Bowmont Valley and on to the Tweed at Kelso would be clear. If they moved the cows briskly, they would certainly be down off the hills without much delay.

Whatever decision Geordie Burn made, it was the wrong one. Driving stolen beasts before them, he and his men blundered into a patrol led by Sir Robert Carey, Warden of the English East March.

With perhaps twenty troopers at his back, Carey did not hesitate to attack. In a sharp fight, two reivers were killed, one of them Jock Burn. Another spurred his pony and escaped, while Geordie was taken prisoner.

It was routine work for Carey and his men and precisely what their patrols were intended to achieve – the interception of raids and the apprehending of raiders. And Burn was no especially prized prisoner. Not a noblemen or a heidsman, he was the client of Sir Robert Ker of Cessford. Nevertheless, Carey understood Border politics well and once Burn had been incarcerated, probably in Harbottle Castle, he made sure that news reached Cessford Castle, the Ker stronghold between Jedburgh and Kelso. Perhaps an exchange might be possible or some other advantage gained? In the event, Burn cannot have been of sufficient status or interest to Ker and no word came back over the hill trails to Carey at Harbottle. The reiver had been left to his fate – an agonising, choking death at the end of a rope.

And then, this routine story became remarkable. The 16th-century Border country was much coloured by the criminal society created by the reivers and, because English records were far better kept than Scottish, there are good descriptions of these horse-riding thieves and the damage they did. But they did not speak for themselves. Unlike Robert Carey, they did not leave diaries. A sense of what and how these men thought, what their attitudes were, is very difficult to discover – except in the case of Geordie Burn.

With two companions, Carey went to visit the condemned man. In the flicker of candlelight, Burn spoke of his life and his crimes. It is almost certainly a unique testimony. Carey's diary entry on the whole incident is worth quoting at length as it represents a snapshot of how the criminal society of the late 16th century worked. Ker is rendered as Car and Burn as Bourne.

> There was a favourite of Sir Robert Car's, a great thief, called Geordie Bourne. This gallant, with some of his associates, would in

a bravery come and take goods in the East March. I had that night some of the garrison abroad. They met with this Geordie and his fellows, driving of cattle before them. The garrison set upon them, and with a shot killed Geordie Bourne's uncle, and he himself, bravely resisting, till he was sore hurt in the head, was taken. After he was taken, his pride was such as he asked who it was that durst avow that night's work? But when he heard it was the garrison, he was then more quiet. But so powerful and awful was this Sir Robert Car and his favourites, as there was not a gentleman in all the East March that durst offend them. Presently after he was taken, I had most of the gentleman of the March come to me, and told me that now I had the ball at my foot, and might bring Sir Robert Car to what condition I pleased; for that this man's life was so near and dear unto him, as I should have all that my heart could desire for the good and quiet of the country and myself, if upon any condition I would give him his life. I heard them and their reasons; notwithstanding, I called a jury the next morning, and he was found guilty of March treason. Then they feared that I would cause him to be executed that afternoon, which made them come flocking to me, humble intreating me that I would spare his life till the next day: and if Sir Robert Car came not himself to me, and made me not such proffers as I could not but accept, that then I should do with him what I pleased. And further, they told me plainly that if I should execute him before I had heard from Sir Robert Car, they must be forced to quit their houses and fly the country; for his fury would be such against me and the March I commanded, as he would use all his power and strength to the utter destruction of the East March. They were so earnest with me that I gave them my word he should not die that day. There was post upon post sent to Sir Robert Car; and some of them rode to him themselves to advertise him in what danger Geordie Bourne was: how he was condemned, and should have been executed that afternoon, but by their humble suit I gave them my word that he should not die that day; and therefore besought him that he would send to me with all the speed he could, to let me know that he would be the next day with me, to offer me good conditions for the safety of his life. When all things were quiet, and the watch set at night, after supper, about ten of the clock, I took one of my men's liveries, and put it about me, and took two other of my servants with me in their liveries, and we three, as the Warden's men, came to the Provost Marshal's, where Bourne was, and were let into his chamber. We sat down by him, and told him that we were desirous to see him, because we heard that he was stout and valiant, and true to his friend; and that we were sorry our master could not be moved to save his life. He voluntarily of himself said, that he had lived long enough to do so many villanies as he had done; and withal told us that he had lain with above forty men's wives, what in England, what in Scotland; and that he had killed seven Englishmen with his own hands, cruelly murdering them: that he had spent his whole time in whoring, drinking, stealing, and taking deep revenge for slight offences. He seemed to be very penitent, and much desired a minister for the comfort of his soul. We promised him to let our master know his desire, who, we knew, would presently grant it. We took our leaves of him; and presently I took order that Mr. Selby, a very worthy honest preacher, should go to him, and not stir from him till his execution the next morning: for after I had heard his own confession, I was resolved no conditions should save his life; and so took order that at the gates opening the next morning he should be carried to execution, which accordingly was performed.

Carey's was amongst the very earliest autobiographies to be written in English and his style is admirable, fresh, direct and insightful. And what is immediately striking is the reaction of the 'gentlemen' of the English East March to Burn's capture and looming death sentence. 'For the good and quiet of the country, and myself,' they pleaded, let him live. Such was the power of these interlocking criminal relationships, very reminiscent of the Italian Mafia, that the potential vengeance of Burn's patron, Sir Robert Ker, far outweighed the justice of the sentence. Which is remarkable since the reiver had probably stolen cows belonging to one of more of the gentlemen who wanted to see clemency or at least delay. And, when Carey went on, very properly, to have Burn convicted, there was near panic as the gentlemen came 'flocking'. Wisely, the March Warden did delay the carrying-out of the sentence so that messages could cross the Cheviots. Indeed, some of the terrified English landowners saddled their own ponies to ride and tell Ker themselves about his man's predicament and, no doubt, seek assurances about the security of their own properties if reprisals were in the heidsman's mind.

But there was silence from Cessford. Apparently Ker would not lift a finger, the conviction for March treason stood and Burn would hang in the morning. Wardens wielded considerable power as they administered the particularly harsh justice of the Borders, using what was known as 'the Laws of the Marches'. On either side of the frontier there were six officials, each one mirroring the other. There were Scottish and English Wardens of the East March, the Middle March and the West March but their behaviour and attitudes were very different. By and large, the English wardens (with the glorious exception of old Sir John Forster, surely the model for Shakespeare's Falstaff), like Robert Carey, were government appointments agreed in London and most men were career soldiers or diplomats in the service of the English monarchs. On the Scottish side, wardenships tended to be inherited or were contended for between rival families. Both the Kers and the Homes held the East March and, in the west, the Maxwells saw the office as their birthright.

Equally striking is Burn's charge sheet – what he confessed to on the evening of his execution. For such a relatively unexceptional professional criminal, he had raped forty women, killed seven Englishmen and spent his time 'whoring, drinking, stealing and taking deep revenge for slight offences'. This last is revealing. If anyone was daft enough to look at Burn in the wrong way, he or she would suffer badly – again, it was reminiscent of the petulance and touchiness of so-called 'men of honour'. The Burns were also known to act wildly disproportionately. In the 1590s, they had murdered no fewer than fourteen men of the English surname of Collingwood in revenge for the death of only one of their own.

Across the farms, towns and villages of Teviotdale and Tweeddale, there must have been scores of men like Geordie Burn. Ordinary people lived in an atmosphere of constant fear, keeping their eyes averted as gangs of these individuals rode or walked past. Life must often have been miserable if, as seems likely, thugs like Burn and his associates behaved entirely without regard for the law or even natural justice.

The sole resort in these dark times was family. For protection, most people probably aligned themselves with a surname and its heidsman, offering services and goods or cash. Even Burn had done so with Sir Robert Ker although, in September 1596, his loyalty was not reciprocated. After the end of reiver society, as romance began to swirl around those intrepid horsemen who rode the moonlight – the ghostly raiders of the superb poetry of Will H. Ogilvie – the effect of reiving on the majority of Borderers can be easily forgotten. In reality, the 16th century, 'the Riding Times', was a time not of stirring derring-do but of terror and frequent destruction.

The stability that was needed to build a productive agrarian economy on both sides the Tweed was rarely sustained. Repeated episodes of invasion and raid in pursuit of the dynastic ambitions of the Tudor kings and queens in particular trailed devastation, fire and misery through the countryside. When armies might tramp up the north road at any time, devouring crops and beasts like locusts, many must have wondered what the point of farming was. In some measure, reiving was a response to all that fearful uncertainty – a brutally direct means of survival. But it also became a downward spiral that led to long periods of near anarchy when spears and swords spoke and the law was silent.

Geordie Burn's confession appears to have been the conscious effort of a condemned man to talk his way if not out of his extreme situation, then perhaps around it. Reivers were famed for their ability to negotiate and Burn seems to have been trying to discover what the terms of a deal with God might be or at least what His church might have to say. Even in 1596, a generation after the Reformation, confession before death, the listing of offences to be taken into consideration, might dampen the fires of damnation a little.

Despite an unbalanced impression, the fact that the much more complete English records tell more about the actions of the Scottish reivers such as Geordie Burn, life was little better south of the Cheviots. There were plenty of local thugs in England. Here is an extract from a letter from the Bishop of Carlisle to Cardinal Wolsey in the 1520s. It is eloquent about how Hexham had become a frontier town:

> [T]here is more theft, more extortion by English thieves than there is by all the Scots of Scotland . . . for in Hexham . . . every market day there is four score or a hundred strong thieves; and the poor men and gentlemen also see those who did rob them and their goods, and dare neither complain of them by name, nor say one word to them. They take all their cattle and horse, their corn as they carry it to sow, or to the mill to grind, and at their houses bid them deliver what they have or they shall be fired and burnt.

The ruins of two solutions to regular raiding can be seen in many parts of the Borders countryside, north and south of the Cheviots. Bastle houses were more common in Northumberland and Cumberland and, while some have been restored and converted into sturdy houses, like the one in a corner of the old Roman fort at High Rochester, others are bramble-covered rickles of stones or stand windy and isolated in the open moorland. Bastles were heavily fortified houses whose ground floors were used to keep cattle safe if a band of raiders appeared on the horizon. With no windows and stout doors secured from the inside, they were difficult for a group of horsemen to prise open. The owners of the cattle cowered on the first floor with all battened down, hoping fervently that their massive stonework and their elevation would protect them.

More common in Teviotdale and Tweeddale were what are known as 'peel towers'. The name is also derived from *palus*, the Latin word for 'a stake', and it refers to the fence around the courtyard, the successor of a bailey. Perhaps the most splendid peel tower stands on its crag outside the village of Smailholm, near Kelso. It commands wide views to the south, the direction most of the trouble came from, and it has been wonderfully well restored. Towers were expensive to build but easy to defend. Sir Thomas Carleton was Deputy Warden of the English West March but also a noted reiver. He left a record of a raid on a tower in Scotland.

Lying on an island of higher ground in the midst of a treacherous moss, Lochwood Tower was a stronghold of the Johnstones, a powerful surname in the West March. Carleton had intelligence that, although the tower was well built and appointed, it was defended by only a few men and some servants. When the English raiders arrived at the edge of the moss, they dismounted and a small group crept towards the tower. It was late afternoon in the winter of 1547 and there was enough light in the sky for Carleton and his men to avoid the pools and sucking mud of the bog. When the early dark came, the reivers slipped over the wall of the courtyard or *barnekin* and 'stole into the house within the barnekin and took the wenches and kept them secure in the house till daylight'. The serving girls must have been terrified as they were bound and gagged and perhaps worse.

Carleton discovered from the wenches that there were only two men and a kitchen maid in Lochwood itself. When the morning sun melted down the Moffatdale Hills in the morning, the reivers looked out of the windows for signs of life in the tower above. Such was the

he Mote, photographed in 1912

uld Mid Raw, demolished in 1884

Hawick Common Riding, 1902, led by Cornet William N. Graham

Hawick Railway Station, 1903

cavalry regiment at Stobs Camp, 1904

tobs Camp Post Office and a group of regimental postmen, 1905

The unveiling of The Horse by Lady Sybil Scott in June 1914

The 400th anniversary celebrations of Hornshole in 1914 at the Volunteer Park. Miss Margot Barclay, 'the Queen of the Borderland', is drawn in her 'car' by 21 pages

he Chase

n autographed portrait of the great Jimmy Guthrie

Manly support – made in Hawick

Jimmy Guthrie's characteristic riding style

Jack Anderson, Hawick and Scotland, Huddersfield and Great Britain. The only Scot ever to score two tries against the All Blacks

:awick RFC, Border and Scottish Champions, 1959–60

Bill McLaren

design that it could be held by only two defenders and they needed the door at ground level to be opened from the inside. After a time, one of the men appeared on the wall walk at the top of the tower, 'wearing a sark', no doubt yawning and stretching. He shouted down to the servant lass to open the door. That was the moment Carleton and his men had been waiting for – but it almost went wrong. 'Our men in the barnekin broke a little too soon.' The girl saw them running from the house and almost got the door shut before the first reiver's shoulder slammed into it.

In the early 16th century, peel towers were raised all over the Borders and not only on defensible sites in the countryside like Lochwood and Smailholm but also in towns. Old maps of Jedburgh show that a tower once stood near the Mercat Cross. In Hawick, what is sometimes known as 'The Black Tower of Drumlanrig' was built east of the confluence of the Slitrig and the Teviot, no doubt to control the crossing. Its location hints that the village had spread beyond its early limits, moving out of the hedge farm, the defences of the ditch and the rivers. Originally an L-shaped structure, the tower resembles the one at Greenknowe near Gordon. With its only entrance in the re-entrant angle, Drumlanrig's Tower was strongly built from greywacke – a coarse, dark local sandstone – and, unusually in the history of such fortifications, it seems never to have been burned. And, although this is difficult to establish in a built environment, it is likely that, for the early period of its history, there would have been a barnekin courtyard. When archaeologists dug trenches close to the tower in March 1989, they discovered traces of a ditch and bank, similar to what had been dug around the bailey up at Hawick Moat. In a posthole found between the ditch and the walls of the tower, a telltale sherd of pottery was retrieved. Known as 'Gritty Ware', it formed part of a jug and the archaeologists dated it to the later 12th century or the early 13th.

Now, this is significant. The ditch, its bank and the posthole and its post could have had any number of uses but their proximity to the

16th-century tower is surely very suggestive. Did the Lovels move downhill and cross the Slitrig to build a new and more comfortable fortification, perhaps a stone-built forerunner of the present building? It seems very likely.

The Black Tower of the Douglases had three storeys and a garret. The basement of the main block of the L-shape was vaulted and, like the smaller bastle houses across the border, it may have been used to keep beasts safe when bands of raiders were prowling the countryside. On the first floor was the hall, the heartbeat of the tower, where business was done, meetings held, meals taken and where retainers slept on straw palliasses or wherever was comfortable – nearest the fire, probably. Above the hall were smaller chambers, sleeping quarters for lords and ladies.

In the re-entrant angle, which faced south-west, the entrance to the Black Tower was guarded by two gun loops cut into the walls of each angle of the L-shape. Defenders could also run quickly upstairs to the wall-walk, parts of which were rediscovered by archaeologists in 1992. There was a parapet that offered those on the wall-walk some protection from archers.

Drumlanrig's Tower is a deceptive building, its original layout having been hidden for centuries. In 1701–02, it was converted to make a townhouse for the redoubtable Anna, the first Duchess of Buccleuch. Her builders filled in the re-entrant angle to make a broadly square house, essentially what has survived until the present day. Anna was a fascinating and formidable figure. Also Duchess of Monmouth, her husband was James Crofts, the eldest but illegitimate son of Charles II. As Duke of Monmouth, he was much loved and favoured by his royal father but, when the Catholic James II succeeded, rebellion flared. Monmouth led the army defeated at the battle at Sedgemoor in July 1685 and he was executed soon afterwards on Tower Hill in London. Anna was at first imprisoned but she used all her contacts, diplomatic skill and grit to ensure the continuation of the Buccleuch title and its holdings. In 1700, she came north and, at Hawick, had her townhouse fashioned out of the Black Tower. Perhaps her experiences drew her to the dour solidity of the old Douglas stronghold.

In 1769, the Tower became a famous coaching inn on the busy route between Edinburgh and Carlisle. When stagecoaches clattered under the old arch, they pulled up at stables where the horses could be changed. Travellers could find food, drink and rest at the inn before they carried on the shoogly and slow journey up the Teviot to Mosspaul and down into Ewesdale. Latterly, the coaching inn and the stables were run by the Croall family. Their express stagecoach service only ended with the death of John Croall in 1873. For a century longer, until the 1980s, Croall Bryson ran a garage on the site of the old stables and the Tower Hotel itself closed in 1985.

The need for secure peel towers was constantly underlined in the 16th century as international politics sent armies north in pursuit of Tudor ambitions. The most severe phases of raiding took place between the 1520s and the 1540s. Tremendous damage was done to the Border abbeys, Kelso in particular. But all of that misery was not triggered by the defeat at Flodden in 1513 and the subsequent weakness of the Scottish monarchy. The seeds of the criminal society of the Border Reivers had been sown over decades before James IV marched south. To the south-west of Hawick, two isolated valleys had become home to notorious bands of horse-riding thieves and, in the years before the disaster at Flodden, their raids regularly found their way into the historical record.

The River Lyne runs into the Esk near Gretna, only a mile or so before its outfall into the Solway, but it reaches back into wild hill country, rising in the moors north of the Roman outpost fort at Bewcastle in what is now the Kielder Forest. The reiving families who lived there were labelled 'the traitors of Levyn' and Teviotdale was a favourite target. They appear to have acted as mercenaries or enforcers in local quarrels. Walter Scott of Howpasley was indicted for bringing the traitors of Levyn to burn Harehead and, in 1510, John Dalglish was convicted of hiring 'Black John Routlesche and his accomplices, traitors of Levyn, to the burning of Branxholme, and the herschip [theft] of horses, oxen, grain and other goods'. With the help of a band of Armstrongs, they appear to have ridden as far west as Ancrum, trailing destruction and outrage in their wake. David Scott of Stirkschawis or Stirches brought both Armstrongs 'and the traitors of Levyn to the burning of certain houses and horses at Craigend of Mynto'.

Liddesdale was the resort of several notorious reiving surnames who were active before Flodden. To the south-west of Liddesdale and into Eskdale, Ewesdale and Wauchopedale, the Armstrongs were immensely powerful and numerous. Their heidsman could put 3,000 men in the saddle in a morning – a small but dangerous and highly mobile army. The Elliots held Upper Liddesdale, nearest Hawick, but other surnames rode wherever gain could be easily achieved. In a series of shifting alliances, Nixons, Bells, Croziers, Irvines, Littles and Batesons saddled their ponies to follow the Elliot or Armstrong captains. And, just as in Hexham, gangs of these thugs walked the streets of Hawick as law-abiding, fearful folk hurried by, their eyes downcast.

And, by the early 16th century, there were streets. By the time the Black Tower was built and the status of a burgh of barony granted, the village had become more substantial. One source has counted 110 houses in addition to St Mary's and a mill on the Slitrig near where the later corn mill buildings survive. When Auld Mid Raw was finally pulled down in 1884 to create spacious Drumlanrig Square, its eleven three-storey houses had been home to a staggering 171 people. The census of 1861 reckoned an average of between fifteen and sixteen inhabitants to each house. In the early 16th century few, if any, of the 110 houses in Hawick will have been built of stone or had more than a ground floor. Nevertheless, a rough calculation might put the population of the village at something like 600 souls.

They suffered both from local reivers from the valleys to the south-west and from the depredations of English raids. Both parties appeared to act with impunity in the power vacuum created by the weakness of Scottish central authority. But, in 1528, decisive action was at last taken.

Before a parliament convened in Edinburgh, Scott of Buccleuch, the Kers of Cessford and Ferniehurst, Maxwell from the West March, Home from the East, Johnstone and other leading heidsmen were all summoned, immediately arrested and imprisoned. Thieves from Ettrick and Yarrow, William Cockburn of Henderland and Adam Scott of Tushielaw were summarily executed and their heads spitted on spikes outside the Edinburgh Tolbooth in the High Street. Scott had the epithet 'King of Thieves' attached to notice of his death. One of his many crimes was the taking of blackmail, something of a reiver speciality. Its meaning in the 16th century was more like protection money. If cash or goods were handed over, Scott and others promised to protect a farmer's stock from other thieves. If it was not, they would lift the cows themselves. But, despite these brisk actions, the real king of thieves was still at large in the Borders. James V was determined once again to act decisively.

In the summer of 1528, the king led a military expedition to part of his own kingdom. Eight thousand strong, his soldiers advanced into Upper Teviotdale and halted at Carlenrig, about ten miles south-west of Hawick. A meeting had been arranged.

After their arrest in Edinburgh, the Border heidsmen had provided assurances of good behaviour and guarantees that men of their surname would cease reiving. That was valuable but incomplete. The greatest reiver of all had not appeared at the parliament in Edinburgh and so the king had come to the Borders to meet him. Black Jock was how his contemporaries knew him and Johnnie Armstrong of Gilnockie is how history and romantic fable remember him.

Carlenrig lies just off the A7. Close to the main road stands a well-set kirk and opposite, a kirkyard that contains something remarkable, a solemn memorial to a murderer and a thief. Tradition holds that James V met Johnnie Armstrong at Carlenrig in the summer of 1530 and that the reiver was betrayed. The Rev. George Ridpath's authoritative *Border History* reported the incident very pithily when he wrote that the king caused '48 banditti to be hanged on growing trees' and that John Armstrong was amongst them. That is all. And yet the incident almost immediately began to be elaborated and its importance enhanced by the swirl of romance. What really happened, however, is likely to be more interesting than the tales, ballads and eventually the plays written about the bold Johnnie Armstrong.

Assurances must have been given for a meeting at Carlenrig to go ahead. Armstrong was too long in the tooth, too much of a practised criminal to walk into a trap, and it appears that he was indeed betrayed – but not in a premeditated manner. The key to understanding the incident is the phrase much repeated in the sources that the Armstrongs were hanged on 'growing trees' or 'growand trees'. The tales and ballads do more than hint at Black Jock as a bold, well-dressed, perhaps cocky man and James V was only seventeen years old in 1530. It may be that tempers frayed and that the young king summarily condemned the reivers and had them hanged there and then. On growand trees. As his advisors no doubt insisted, a scaffold in Edinburgh or Jedburgh would have been better as the conclusion of due process, the rule of law. Lynching 48 banditti at Carlenrig was little better behaviour than that of the reivers themselves and a show trial would have had a much greater impact.

It may indeed have been the case that Johnnie Armstrong was ill done to and that, in turn, sparked the largely sympathetic literature that followed his execution. There was a dark glamour, a Jack-the-Lad playfulness, a memory of style and dash. The reality, of course, was much different and the incident had little impact on the behaviour of the Armstrongs. Johnnie's elder brother, Sim the Laird, was still active and dangerous.

Royal expeditions to the Borders continued. In 1567, James Stewart, the Earl of Moray, had been appointed regent after the abdication of Mary Queen of Scots. Her son, James VI, was only a little boy.

Having received good intelligence about the movements and habits of Liddesdale reivers, Moray mustered a small force with Lords Lindsay and Home. Probably on a market day, they suddenly surrounded the village of Hawick and captured forty reivers. As a crowd gathered, some of these men, perhaps Elliots and Armstrongs amongst them, had their hands tied behind their backs. They were dragged down to the pools where the Slitrig and Teviot join and, one by one, they were drowned. It was important that even rough justice like this was seen to be done and Moray's soldiers may have forced people to watch from the banks and the bridge as the reivers' heads were thrust into the water and held down as they wriggled and kicked. Other arrested reivers, having no doubt watched the procession of drownings, were taken off to trial in Edinburgh.

By the 1570s, Hawick was firmly in the possession of the Scotts of Buccleuch in what would quickly prove a dangerous lease. Regent Moray was murdered in 1570 and a succession of brief regencies followed. Chaos and uncertainty in Edinburgh was meat and drink to the Border Reivers and the Scotts and the Kers of Cessford in particular rode hard and often over the border to lift cattle and goods. Elizabeth I of England was apparently incandescent with rage, and if the Scottish monarchy could not control the Borders, then she would. Under the command of the Earl of Sussex, an English army of 5,000 crossed the frontier at the Reddenburn, bypassed Kelso and burned a Scott tower at Eckford and a Ker stronghold near Crailing before keeping a rendezvous with the men of the English Middle March and the Warden, Old Sir John Forster. One of the most attractive characters of the 16th century, this old rogue lived until he was 101 and held the Middle March Wardenry for forty years, wheeling, dealing and stealing as he did so.

Once the two armies had combined and laid plans, they advanced on the Scott town of Hawick. As they rode up the Teviot, scouts could see smoke billowing into the sky and, by the time they reached Cavers, it looked as though the town was ablaze. The presence of the large English army at Jedburgh had been reported widely and, forewarned, the townspeople had hauled the thatch off their roofs and burned it in the streets. The skeletons of stone or wood and wattle walls were much harder to fire. When destroying a town or village, soldiers always lit the thatch and the prudent Hawick folk had denied them their firelighters. Having piled all of their moveable goods into the Black Tower or taken with them what was portable, they also fled into the hills with every sack and scrap of food. Beasts were probably already grazing out on the town's common. Sussex's men were forced to rely on their own rations and what they could pillage from house gardens. For some unknown reason, they did not fire the Tower. Perhaps they tried and failed.

Meanwhile James VI was growing up and Elizabeth I was growing old. And childless. By the late 1580s and into the 1590s, it became increasingly clear that James VI would become James I of Great Britain and Ireland. A great prize but one that could be denied if those opposed at the English court could legitimately point out that the Scottish king could not control his own subjects in the Borders, far less rule over the English, the Welsh and the Irish. Pressure to curb reiving and bring the riding surnames in from the periphery was mounting. And, more than that, the heidsmen knew that the world was changing. If James became King of England, the border would mean much less and their ability to play off one jurisdiction against another would be at an end. But there was time yet for one last raid – perhaps the greatest of them all.

On 17 March 1596, a truce day was in progress at Kershopefoot in Liddesdale. These meetings had been set up to deal with cross-border complaints and those who came to answer them or make them were guaranteed immunity. Kinmont Willie Armstrong had ridden the moonlight for more than forty years and been a constant thorn and threat to the Warden of the English West March, Lord Scrope. By 1596, Scrope's son had succeeded and inherited the family hatred of Willie. At Kershopefoot, this spilled over into illegality. Contrary to march law, English soldiers seized Willie on his way home after the truce day and dragged him off to imprisonment and trial at Carlisle Castle. What followed was perhaps the best-planned, most classic raid in reiving history.

Walter Scott of Buccleuch was the Keeper of Liddesdale, a sub-wardenry over the wildest men on the Border, and he wrote to Lord Scrope pointing out that he had acted illegally and requested the release of Armstrong. No reply. Another letter. No reply. Plans were laid. Carlisle is a dour lump of a castle, very difficult to breach by siege and impossible for a band of reivers to break into. Inside knowledge and collusion was needed. The Carletons had been Deputy March Wardens and the son of the man who took Lochwood Tower, another Thomas Carleton, had a grievance. Lord Scrope had sacked him. Contact was made, cash produced and a date set. The raid would run on the night of Sunday 13th of April.

It was much better for Walter Scott to lead a small force able to move quickly and only 80 or so could do the job. And so, at Langholm Races on Saturday 12th of April, they mustered, taking care not to be obvious. The following morning Buccleuch and his men slipped out of the town on the Carlisle road. When they reached Stanwix Bank, west of the city, it was raining and the River Eden was in flood. Records note that 'it happened to be very dark in the hindnight [after midnight] and a little misty' – good cover – and, as the riders moved behind the screen of Stanwix Bank, they approached the swollen river. A crossing would take good horsemanship and brave ponies.

Soaked but across, Buccleuch led his men to a postern gate. The Carletons had told them where Kinmont was being held and, when they broke in, amazingly, there were no guards to be seen. Too wet, nobody would be about anyway in such foul weather, and better to count the Carletons' coins by the light of a warming fire than venture out on to the walls. Once Armstrong had been bundled on to a pony and the raiders had splashed and swum the Eden, they rode like a night wind for the Border. And got clean away.

It was a last, triumphant hurrah for a way of life that was already fading into the darkness of the past. When Old Queen Bess finally died in 1603 and Robert Carey rode like a man possessed for Edinburgh to tell James VI the news he had been waiting for all his life, the world of the reivers changed. The heidsmen knew it. In an orgy of raiding triggered by the news during what was immediately dubbed 'Ill Week', Armstrongs, Grahams, Elliots and others lifted 5,000 head of cattle in Cumbria. One party of reivers led by Hutcheon Graham rode brazenly under the walls of Carlisle watched by the bishop. Perhaps they raised two fingers to him. But, when James VI began his progress to his coronation in London, he paused in Newcastle to issue a stern proclamation:

> To his messengers, sheriffs and others, the late marches of the two realms of England and Scotland are now the heart of the country. Proclamation is to be made against all rebels and disorderly persons that no supply be given them, their wives or their bairns, and that they be prosecuted with fire and sword.

Having firmly taken control of the reins of government in London a few weeks later, the new king once more addressed himself to the riding surnames, noting the excesses of Ill Week.

> Requiring all who were guilty of the foul and insolent outrages lately committed in the Borders to submit themselves to his mercy before 20th June – under penalty of being excluded from it forever . . . [the king] prohibited the name of Borders any longer to be used, substituting in its place Middle Shires. He ordered all places of strength in those parts to be demolished except the habitation of noblemen and barons; their iron yetts to be converted into plough irons and their inhabitants to betake themselves to agriculture and other works of peace.

Aye, right. Some heidsmen may have smirked at the royal renaming of their territory. Middle Shires indeed! But the intention to pacify and bring the Borders back into a law-abiding world was translated quickly into action. In 1605, a Border Commission was set up in Carlisle Castle and it did not waste time. Hang them was the usual conclusion. The concept of Jethart Justice was not born in 1605 but it was certainly pursued and, by 1610, most of the leading reivers had been imprisoned, hanged, deported or ennobled. A peace of sorts descended at last on the Borders. Mosstroopers still prowled the hill trails but organised crime had been largely snuffed out. Well-known thieves no longer strutted the streets of Hexham or Hawick. The world had at last moved on.

6

CORNETS, THE COMMON AND CARTERHAUGH

HAWICK GREW very slowly after the reiving times. In the wars that followed the rift between Charles I and his parliament – what is often miscalled the English Civil War (it affected Scotland and Ireland profoundly) – the Solemn League and Covenant was signed in 1643 by Scottish Covenanters and the English parliamentary party. Deeply anti-royalist and anxious to maintain the independence of the Church of Scotland, the Lords of the Covenant raised an army and demanded that each Scottish burgh supply soldiers to fight for the common cause. The ratio was set at one soldier for every 60 inhabitants and, according to the town records, Hawick could supply only ten. That means that, in 1644, there were probably between 600 and 800 living in the town.

The records also offer the first glimpse, the earliest sense, of the extent and character of the burgh. To the west, a vennel or pathway led from the West Port down to the Teviot where there was a coble ferry – a flat-bottomed raft that could be poled across to the opposite bank at Langlands. The West Port stood at the head of the Auld Mid Raw which, in the 17th century, was flanked by Back and Fore Raws. Early maps show that Fore Raw ran on the south-eastern side of Auld Mid Raw and that the Kirk Wynd turned a right angle, as it does now, down to the Slitrig. Back Raw lay on the other side and the Howegate ran down to the river.

This sort of arrangement of parallel streets survives in Lauder where a block of houses tails behind the old town hall or tollbooth and streets run either side. From the Back Raw, the Howegate ran down to the Sandbed and the Slitrig where what was called the Garrison or the Lieutenant's Tower stood. Close by was the Auld Brig over the Slitrig, what linked the older, western part of Hawick with the High Street and the more recently built area. Known respectively as Eastla and Westla, each part of the town used to take turns to elect the early Hawick Cornets.

In front of the Black Tower was Tower Knowe and it overlooked the haughland down by the banks of the Teviot. On this hillock, there once stood a tall tree. It was probably the Devil's Tree, the prominent place where those convicted of crimes by the bailies – the town magistrates – were forced to stand and endure public humiliation. Opposite the Black Tower was the town mill and it was apparently defended by another fortified building, perhaps a tower. The High Street ran westwards but had a short central row of houses, echoing the arrangement across the Slitrig. The market cross and the Tolbooth – the town hall and prison – stood where the stately 19th-century town hall now rises.

Criminals, often guilty of petty offences, were also made to stand at the mercat cross with notes pinned to them detailing their offences and often items they stole were hung around their necks. One Hawick woman had helped herself to her neighbour's peat and had clods placed on her shoulders, another had taken a pan and it was hung around her neck. There seem to have been stocks at the Tolbooth and those convicted by the bailies were locked into them. Inside the steeple of St Mary's fetters had been built into the wall and there are records of men being secured there to await trial. One man, John Elliot, contrived to commit suicide while locked into the fetters. Apparently he hanged himself with his belt and, in the morning, his body was found 'deid in the irnes'.

Punishments for even minor offences could be very severe. Two petty thieves, Margaret Drummond and Elizabeth Miller, were 'whipped and scourged' through the streets of Hawick and, at the Tolbooth, they were held down while an H was branded on to their cheeks. The eastern boundary of the town lay just beyond the mercat cross and a plaque marks the location of the East Port near what is now Brougham Place. It has been fixed above the Waverley Bar. A few yards further east, Bourtree Place remembers an old custom. Bourtrees or elders were traditional boundary markers and the road to Jedburgh probably passed under a stand of them at some point in Hawick's history.

In 1627, a set of valuation records complained that the town was without a school. At Melrose, Jedburgh and Kelso, the monastic orders had set up medieval grammar schools but there was no equivalent at Hawick. Clearly desirable for practical and educational reasons, the establishment of a parish school was also seen as a benign consequence of the Scottish Reformation. A central tenet of the Reformers was known as 'the priesthood of all believers' and this involved the ability of the mass of people to be able to read the Bible for themselves without relying on the 'mumbo jumbo' of a priest. There would, John Knox and his colleagues declared, be a school in every parish in Scotland and, by the end of the 17th century, their goal had been largely achieved. In Hawick, it seems that £100 would be 'allowed for the maintaining of a scool in this large towne'. And. some time after 1627, it opened its doors to children.

Despite the conclusion of the civil wars and the eventual expulsion of the Stewart dynasty, times remained turbulent. In Galloway in particular but also in the Borders, the faith of the Covenanters endured. Up on Ruberslaw there is an informal monument to that very thrawn, very Scottish piety. Alexander Peden was a charismatic Covenanting minister from Auchinleck in Ayrshire who travelled widely across the south of Scotland to preach outdoors to the faithful. Because of official, often violent, disapproval, congregations met at field conventicles – open-air services. At Gateshaw Braes near

Morebattle anniversaries linked to local dissenting traditions are held out of doors. The last field conventicle was preached in 1989.

Hawick was almost certainly home to a group of Covenanters for, near Ruberslaw's summit, there is an outcrop known as Peden's Pulpit. There are several other places in Scotland with the same name but surely the singular cone of Ruberslaw is the most spectacular. Lookouts no doubt watched for approaching dragoons as Peden preached the true word of God to those in Hawick who followed it. For the sake of anonymity as he moved through the countryside, the notorious Covenanting minister wore a mask which can still be seen in the Royal Museum of Scotland in Edinburgh. Made from linen with eye slits and tufts of hair attached, it looks scary and was more likely to attract attention than deflect it.

In addition to religious dissent, the 17th century also saw disagreements of a more secular and venal nature in the Borders. A gradual erosion of the rights of the burghs to common land had begun as surrounding lords claimed more and more for themselves. Selkirk's vast common of 22,000 acres was seriously whittled down. In 1607 and again in 1656, townspeople fought the bands of the retainers of local lords in order to protect their ancient rights. But, in 1678, the Earl (later Duke) of Roxburgh forced through a division of the South Common that gave him large tracts of land around Bowden and Whitmuir. An act of the Scottish Parliament in 1695 formalised this and other land grabs. Common ridings were never more important.

In 1703 or 1705 (authorities differ), the name of the Hawick Cornet was first recorded. He was James Scott 'called Laird' and his title (and that of his predecessors) was an appropriate military rank. In the cavalry regiments of the British army until 1871, a Cornet was the most junior officer, below lieutenant and captain. But, crucially, the Cornet carried the regimental colours – he was the standard bearer. The Hawick town flag, the famous banner blue, was certainly used at that time in the history of the Common Riding because the Cornet of 1706 refused to carry it. It had become very tattered and torn. Money was found to commission a new flag and, in 1707, it was carried by Cornet George Deans. With his supporters, Deans rode the common. Not only did he look like a cavalry officer, he was also well armed. Until 1784, the Cornet, his Right and Left Hand Men and several others took pistols and swords as they rode the bounds.

In 1732, at the great age of 81, Anna, Duchess of Buccleuch died. She had been a steadfast patron of the town, often in residence at the Black Tower (her principal home was at Dalkeith Palace) as she dispensed judgements and offered advice in the hall, sitting on a raised dais under a canopy. The Duchess occasionally interceded on behalf of townspeople who were believed to have been wrongly convicted of serious crimes and, when Hawick began to expand a little, she paid for the paving of the High Street. The Kirk Session at St Mary's recorded a gift of £100 for the poor relief fund. The old duchess had seen Britain and Scotland change dramatically in her long lifetime. Dynasties had fallen and been replaced and the Union of the Parliaments had, in essence, abolished the residual importance of the border in 1707.

Sport emerges from the shadows in the early 18th century and was to grow into an enormously vibrant facet of life in Hawick. Horse racing had been very popular in the time of the reivers and the meeting at Langholm where Buccleuch mustered his raiders was one of several fixtures in the calendar. The oldest horse-racing trophies on record are the Carlisle Bells of 1590 and 1597 and the Peebles Bell is also very old. Meetings were usually held on tracks laid out on high and open moorland sites which had either been close cropped by sheep pasturing or were part of a town's common land or both. The earliest record of horse racing at Hawick Common Riding is for 1723 and the meeting was probably held at the Deidhaugh. The fixture was later moved to the Vertish Hill and horses raced there until 1819. For whatever reason, a site at Pilmuir Rig was then preferred. The modern track first came into use in 1855.

Lang bullets had nothing to do with guns. It was a very popular sport in Hawick and had been played in the High Street since the late

Middle Ages. So popular was it that the priest at St Mary's, one Robert Irland, felt moved to warn the local lads to cease and desist from 'the bowlis'. Lang bullets was diverting them from mandatory archery practice down at the Butts. Slightly better known as road bowls, it was a simple pastime. Using a ball about the size of a modern cricket ball, the idea was to throw it along a road or other reasonable hard surface (so that there was some bounce) towards a fixed object like a tree or a wall. And the winner was whoever reached the fixed object in the fewest throws. The High Street will have been a popular venue after Duchess Anna paid for its paving. Many could compete at the same time but the game declined in the late 18th century when roads began to acquire more traffic. What might be called short bullets – or bowls played on a bowling green – remains popular in Hawick where the prestigious Pow Cup is competed for each year. One of the most distinguished and skilful winners in the early 20th century was William Irvine of Allars Crescent.

The reivers played lang bullets as well as shooting them. They also raced their ponies and their other passion was football. Willie Armstrong and the Earl of Bothwell (husband of Mary Queen of Scots) were keen players in what appears to have been very robustly contested matches. The score after one played near Carlisle was said to have been two dead and thirty taken prisoner. In the early 18th century, fitba' began to change from a game where the ball and opponents were kicked to one where players picked it up and began to run with it or compete for it in a scrummage. Rugby was beginning to evolve.

The origins of the game described as 'Hawick's religion' stretch back in time long before the fabled day in the winter of 1823 when William Webb Ellis is said to have picked up a football at a match at Rugby School and run with it. 'Ba' or 'handba' was played in various versions all over Western Europe and, in the 18th century, it was popular in Hawick, Hobkirk, Denholm, St Boswells and Ancrum and was played as late as the 1930s at Lilliesleaf. The old game survives gloriously in Jedburgh and is played once a year in Duns. The rules, such as they are, appear to be similar, at least in spirit, although they have never been published, so it can be difficult to check, but perhaps that is the point – the arguments being half the fun.

Jethart Ba is played twice a year between two teams of men – the Uppies and the Doonies. The names are illogical but precise and anyway everyone in Jed understands who belongs where. And that is all that matters. The Callants' Ba is played at Candlemass in early February and the Men's Ba on Fastern's E'en or Shrove Tuesday, as it is known elsewhere. When a stitched leather ba stuffed with straw or moss and with ribbons attached is thrown up into the air at the Mercat Cross, the game begins, usually with a huge scrummage. Teams can be 200 strong. Sometimes a player breaks away with the ba and the idea is to score hails – a bit like tries in modern rugby but not really. For the Uppies, hails are won when the ba is thrown over a particular section of the railings surrounding Jedburgh Castle and, for the Doonies, when the ba is rolled across an invisible burn. Simple.

Hawick handba was certainly played but no records of any games survive before 1842. It may have been based on the Jethart version and its matches were also held on Shrove Tuesday. As in Jedburgh, Duns and elsewhere, two teams from different parts of the town were involved. Since the Eastla and Westla division was considered important enough to insist on alternative selections for Cornet, it seems fair to assume that this split was well understood and perhaps time-honoured. It certainly supplied the most readily understood means of dividing Hawick into two teams for handba. It was also even handed. In 1770, a Hawick valuation roll counted 206 houses in the town with 110 noted in the West End and 96 in the 'Eastend'. If Westla meant those born west of the Slitrig or, following the example of Jedburgh, those who lived outside the burgh but who entered it by the West Port, then some correlation with the more modern term of *guitterbluid* is surely possible. The sense of a *guitterbluid* being a person born in the West End, between the two rivers, appears equivalent to

Westla. Eastla is perhaps easier – all those born east of the Slitrig or who enter Hawick by the East Port.

Matches were played along the banks of the Teviot and hails could be scored by the Eastla team by plunging into the river (in February) at the Old Toll at the west end of the Under Haugh, where the new bridge crossed the river. The Common Haugh, what remains open ground and a handy car park today, had, by that time, become known as the Common Haugh. The Westla team could score by getting the ball into the water at the old town boundary. It ran a little to the north of where the footbridge is now. The 1850s and the railway brought change to Hawick and the handba pitch was adjusted to suit. Hails for the Eastlas were scored further west at the Cobble Cauld and, for the Westlas, at the new railway bridge across the Teviot. Two excellent photographs from 1904 and 1906 show large crowds watching the action and, perhaps not surprisingly, many fewer splashing around in the chill waters of Teviot.

Sometimes as many as six games of the ba could be played on Shrove Tuesdays and the tradition endured late, lasting until the Second World War. Perhaps its dangerous and eccentric nature brought the Hawick ba to an end. There were, reputedly, serious injuries and even drownings and one year play rose to be conducted over the roofs of the houses on the Sandbed. Play at Mansfield Park, Hawick's rugby ground, will have seemed tame by comparison to the tackles made on cobbles, the scrummages of scores of men and the regular duckings in the Teviot.

Hawick men seem to have had a reputation as good handba players in the early 19th century when the earliest record of the playing of anything resembling rugby appeared in the Borders. In late November of 1815, the Duke of Buccleuch hosted a dinner at the newly rebuilt Bowhill House near Selkirk. As the port was passed around and pipes lit, a plan began to form amongst the guests. There would be a 'football' match of epic proportions. Sir Walter Scott volunteered to plan the ceremonies and the Earl of Home would captain a team drawn from the Ettrick and Yarrow Valleys that would play against a combined side of men from Hawick, Selkirk and Gala. It was to prove a dangerous – and unique – sporting alliance. The date and the venue for the grand game were set. It would be played at Carterhaugh, flat flood-plain ground between the Ettrick and Yarrow to the south east of Bowhill, on Monday the 4th of December.

In the winter darkness of a very cold morning, the Hawick contingent of about 100 young callants mustered, probably at the mercat cross. They then marched out of the East Port and, as the day began to dawn, they walked the twelve miles over Grundistone Heights to Selkirk, a journey that probably took three hours. Once in Selkirk they went to Bailie Clarkson's house to meet their teammates, drink a strong dram of whisky and pin a twig of pine to their bonnets or their shirt fronts. And then, in braw order, they all marched down to the Ettrick Bridge and then on to Carterhaugh where they met the Gala lads.

The huge pitch had been set up like a cheery battlefield. Bands played and a booth dispensed refreshment, no doubt suitable to the winter conditions, paid for by Duke Charles. The shepherds and farmers from Ettrick and Yarrow filed on to the field and formed up in what seemed like battle order. On their bonnets and shirts they wore sprigs of heather. When Duke Charles and his retinue rode down from Bowhill House at 11 a.m., the melodramatic hand of Walter Scott became immediately apparent. The ancient war banner of the Scotts of Buccleuch was unfurled and paraded up and down the lines of the Ettrick and Yarrow men to the stirring accompaniment of bagpipe music and the cheers of two thousand spectators – an amazing turnout on a cold Monday morning in December.

There were almost as many players. When Duke Charles threw the ba high in the air to start the match, just as happens at Jedburgh, he no doubt moved smartly out of the way as a huge scrummage clashed and locked. Two goals, the places where hails could be scored, had been set up at marked-off stretches of the Ettrick and Yarrow, almost a mile apart. The townsmen moved play towards the shepherds' goal when suddenly a Selkirk man, a mason called Rob Hall, broke free with the ba. He sidestepped past several flat-footed shepherds before plunging into the freezing winter river to score a hail. As Hawick, Gala and Selkirk men roared approval, he is said to have stood in midstream holding the sodden ba in the air.

The game was intended to be long – lasting from 11 a.m. to 4 p.m. when darkness would begin to descend. But when half time was called, plots began to hatch. The match was not going to plan – the Ettrick and Yarrow men were on the losing side and the position looked unlikely to improve. Walter Scott, perhaps unwisely, intervened and persuaded the Gala contingent to change sides. It was the first stirrings of an enduring enmity. After the restart, the match started to swing in the opposite direction. Townsmen played handba more often than shepherds and farmers and the Gala men seemed to know what they were doing. A hail was soon scored in the Yarrow by George Brodie of Greatlaws. Dusk fell and the match was declared a draw.

But the Hawick and Selkirk men were not happy. They pursued the Gala contingent as they beat a hasty retreat over the Tweed and there were bloody noses and cracked heads. On his way home to Abbotsford, Walter Scott was unwise enough to go through Selkirk. His carriage was stopped and some rough handling (but not rough words) was probably prevented by the handover of two guineas so that the Selkirk team might take drams at his expense. Meanwhile the Hawick men were walking back through the winter dark grumbling, muttering oaths, plotting two hundred year's worth of revenge on the Gala team. Dirty Gala.

The Carterhaugh match was well documented and certainly important for the development of rugby whose more formal story in Hawick belongs to the second half of the 19th century, when the town had become very different. But the game was also emblematic of a growing division in the Borders in that it was designed as a contest between two distinct groups – townsmen and countrymen. If it was needed, spice was also added by the Hawick men playing against a team supported and sponsored by the Duke of Buccleuch. Sixty years earlier they had contended over something altogether more tangible than the outcome of a handba match.

In 1751, the Scotts of Buccleuch were formally granted the Barony of Hawick. This turned out to mark an important change from a de facto position of ownership. After 1675, Duchess Anna had, in effect, owned much of the land but the Dukes of Buccleuch believed that the assumption of the barony changed the legal position radically so far as the Hawick Common was concerned. In 18th-century Scotland, agricultural improvement was gathering pace and land values were rising. By 1767, lawyers representing the duke had brought an action against the people of Hawick that demanded the common be divided between the burgesses and the Buccleuch tenants who rented the lands around its boundaries. Duke Henry claimed that, as Baron of Hawick, he owned all the lands within it, including the Common. Hawick people had customary rights to use it – but it belonged to him.

Lawyers acting for the town cited the charter of the Douglases in the early 16th century and its subsequent confirmation by Mary Queen of Scots. These documents made it clear, they asserted, that the Common was an outright and unconditional gift to the townspeople. Moreover, the annual common ridings were a regular confirmation that the land belonged to Hawick by right of ancient usage.

The case was inconclusive and no verdict appears to have been forthcoming. But, ten years after Duke Henry's action, in 1777, the town council resurrected it. What prompted this is unclear for the status quo was that the town continued to own the Common. The net effect of the initiative was the loss of about a third of the acreage to the Buccleuchs and their tenants. The Common shrank to a little over a thousand acres. But, by 1777, Hawick was changing fast and the loss of so much land upcountry may have been seen as less important than the retention of common land around the town, especially the haughland by the banks of the Teviot.

7

HARDIE'S HAWICK

HAWICK HAS given birth to her fair share of heroes, from Hornshole to Mansfield Park to Murrayfield and beyond. But one man, neither fiery callant nor talented rugby player, deserves a special place in that pantheon. In 1771, Bailie John Hardie took an initiative that changed Hawick utterly.

Change began in the hills, valleys and fields of Borders farms. The second half of the 18th century saw agriculture across Britain revolutionised and, in the Borders, two native geniuses made great contributions. James Small, a Berwickshire blacksmith, invented the swing plough in the 1760s. Cast entirely in iron with the ploughshare wrought in the now characteristic screwed shape, it replaced the slow and inefficient auld Scots ploo. Able to turn over the furrow slice completely and bury weeds, it could be pulled by one strong horse rather than a team of oxen. Drainage improved and much more land was brought into cultivation. Small's invention was quickly and widely adopted and not only did it change the landscape forever, it made farming into a thriving business. The swing plough also encouraged a much more efficient use of labour. Because of its inability to turn the sod over cleanly, the auld ploo needed a team of people behind it, bashing down clods and pulling out weeds. James Small's brilliant invention needed only one man to direct one or two strong horses and no plough followers. People began to move off the land.

Reaching south from Yetholm deep into the hills, almost to the foot of Cheviot, the Bowmont Valley is deceptively beautiful. In summer, its close-cropped sheep lawns amongst the yellow broom and gorse and its glinting stream are a picture of tranquillity. But, in winter, storms blow deep snow down off the watershed ridges and, in severe weather, lonely farms up the valley can find themselves isolated. And yet, in the later 18th century, James Robson, who farmed at Belford in the Bowmont Valley, placed himself right at the centre of what has become known as the Agricultural Revolution. At Belford, he raised flocks of the old breed of Cheviot sheep, the same tough, short-woolled animals that grazed the medieval sheep ranches of Kelso Abbey. Determined to improve the Cheviots, Robson travelled widely in England until he came across rams he believed might make suitable crosses. At Burton-on-Humber, he bought three big, close-coated sheep from a Mr Mumby and drove them north in a cart on what must have been a stressful journey for both parties.

The results of interbreeding the Lincolnshire rams with the narrow shouldered, native Cheviot ewes were a vast improvement. The lambs were much bigger and the volume of the wool clip rose by 20 per cent. And it was of a markedly finer quality. Writing in 1792, the MP and founder of the Board of Agriculture, Sir John Sinclair, was impressed:

> Perhaps there is no part of the whole island where, at first sight, a fine-wooled breed of sheep is less to be expected than among the Cheviot Hills. Many of the sheep-walks consist of nothing but peat bogs and deep morasses. During winter the hills are covered with snow for two, three and sometimes four months . . . They have a closer fleece . . . which keeps them warmer in the cold weather, and prevents either snow or rain from incommoding them.

The close and fine fleeces of James Robson's North Country Cheviots were much more suited to the production of textiles of all sorts than the coarser wool of the traditional black-faced breed and, by the 1830s, these had all but disappeared from the Border hills.

James Robson and James Small changed farming and consequently both were instrumental in making the remarkable development of Hawick possible in the early 19th century.

In the wake of the Union of the Parliaments of 1707, a well-funded and well-organised body called the Board of Trustees for Manufacture was set up in Scotland. With a budget of £6,000 a year, its remit was to improve woollen and linen production and the Scottish fishing industry. The Board was very effective and, by 1772, more than 20,000 Scots were employed in turning out 13 million yards of linen. Flax or lint was grown around Melrose and weavers in the town produced 33,000 yards annually. But with foreign competition, output began to decline rapidly. In 1784, only 17,792 yards were made in Melrose. With the encouragement of the Board of Trustees, entrepreneurs turned their attention to the production of woollen textiles.

Bailie John Hardie was a senior magistrate on Hawick Town Council as well as a successful merchant with premises in the High Street and, perhaps out of civic responsibility or business acumen or a combination of both, he made the long journey to Glasgow in 1771. Judged by contemporaries as 'a Hawick man of quick talents, and a decided mind', Hardie successfully requested a loan from the Board in Edinburgh. He was forty-nine and it may be that a new business venture appealed to him. In Glasgow, Hardie used the loan to buy four knitting machines or stocking frames. Invented in the late 16th century and continually modified and improved since then, they were powered by a treadle and, in essence, imitated the hand movements of knitters except that the frames carried many more needles. And they could work at least ten times faster. Because it was heavy and exhausting work, knitting frames were usually operated by men. Female family members often spun yarn from cleaned and carded wool.

Hardie employed a blacksmith to set up his frames at his shop at 37 High Street and, at first, all of the work was bespoke. Pairs of stockings or hose were made to order for customers. In the late 18th century, men wore knee breeches and long stockings for their feet and lower legs. Most who ordered pairs from Hardie were sufficiently well off to own a horse and, for riding, breeches were far more suitable than trousers. They still are. The flow of production was rudimentary. Knitters were not paid a wage. Instead they hired the frame, paid Hardie 'house-rent' for oil for a lamp (this could be detailed, close-quarter work needing good light and a lamp was hung behind a glass globe filled with water so that it shone more brightly but was diffused), for needles and perhaps for a boy or a girl to wind the yarn. This job was often done by family members.

Knitters worked no set hours but Saturday was the day of reckoning. Hardie gave out enough yarn to fulfil the orders that had been placed and he paid for the stockings made by the knitters that week. Because of days taken off, the oil lamps often burned late on a Friday night. And because they could jingle coins in their pockets on a Saturday night, the knitters were often to be found in the howffs of Hawick. In fact the stocking-makers' weekend could last until Tuesday or Wednesday morning. At the end of the 18th century, whisky was one shilling and three pence a quart and Hawick measures were famously generous. But the stocking shops were not disorganised. One man was in charge of laying and lighting fires in winter while the 'head stockinger' was often deputed to deliver the weekly output to the warehouse and receive payment. When this was handed over in banknotes to cover several men's earnings, the easiest place to find change and divide up the money was of course a public house.

In his first year of operation, John Hardie's four frames turned out only 200 pairs of stockings but output soon began to rise. In 1772, he took on an apprentice, John Potts, and had five frames clacking away in his shop in the High Street. Six women worked at home spinning yarn and sewing up the seams of the stockings. Production increased to 2,400 pairs a year.

Rivals emerged. In 1772, James Haldane, possibly from Haddington, set up four stocking frames in a house in Auld Mid Raw and, two years later, John Nixon was making hosiery. Hardie responded and, in 1775, he took on an experienced English knitter, William Beck, who could also maintain and repair frames. After two years, Beck branched out on his own and his stocking shop still stands behind 21 High Street. Built around 1800 in an L-shaped plan, the first floor looks very distinctive from the outside because it has a row of six square windows. These were designed to give as much light as possible to a stocking maker's frame. Beck was a popular employer – the only manufacturer who refused to lower wages in the lengthy dispute over output and prices that led to a famous strike in 1817 known as The Lang Stand Oot. In 1808, William Beck's son carried the banner blue as Hawick Cornet.

For reasons of 'family distress', John Hardie decided to retire in 1780. On condition that the stocking frames were moved out of 37 High Street, he agreed a partnership arrangement with John Nixon. He took the frames to new and larger premises in Cross Wynd. And there the business changed once more. Some time between 1780 and 1785, Nixon gave up the bespoke manufacture of pairs of stockings and began to make them for sale on a purely speculative basis. In addition, lambswool, as the finer wool of the North Country Cheviots was known, became the dominant raw material – something made possible by the breeding programme begun by James Robson of Belford. Linen, worsted, cotton and even silk had all been used in the past. By 1791, John Nixon was making 3,500 pairs of lambswool stockings and employing thirteen knitters at Cross Wynd as well as forty-two women spinners, nine seamers, doublers and twiners – a workforce of sixty-five in all. Hosiery manufacture was beginning to industrialise.

Bailie John Hardie died on 22nd December 1800 and was buried, much mourned, in St Mary's kirkyard. In the last few years of his life, another man had revolutionised the Hawick hosiery trade – Napoleon Bonaparte. Since 1793, Britain had been at war with France and both soldiers and sailors needed stockings. By the time Hardie's funeral cortege climbed up to the kirk, there were more than 500 stocking frames working in Hawick and annual output had rocketed to 328,000 pairs. Momentum was maintained and, by 1838, more than a million pairs were made in the Borders.

Terrified by Napoleon's armies, the British government was also badly spooked by the egalitarian politics of the French Revolution that produced this remarkable man. In 1799, the Combination Bill was voted into law by the House of Commons and it prohibited the formation of what were essentially trade unions. After Waterloo and the inevitable downturn in business for stocking makers that followed, this act became important. Cheaper and nastier stockings were knitted in Leicester and Derbyshire so the Hawick hosiers wanted to reduce prices to compete. And they proposed to pass these reductions directly on to the knitters. Tradition holds that the Hawick frame workers met in secret and at night in a smiddy in Back Raw. To avoid arrest and the strictures of the Combination Act, no treasurer of this nascent trade union could be appointed but there were important subscription funds to hold safely and manage. Allegedly, at the end of a meeting, the bag containing the coins was placed on the smiddy anvil and the lamps snuffed out. And then, in the anonymous darkness, one man, no one could see who, took the bag and kept it safe until the next meeting. Not only apocryphal but also illogical (Why would only one definitely honest man reach for the bag?), this tale does underline the fact that the knitters had to meet in secret.

In 1817, John Scot announced a cut of a halfpenny a pair for the stockings he had made in Hawick. The knitters refused to accept it and four were jailed at Jedburgh while their comrades staged a strike – a stand oot. What the employers forgot was that the Combination Act also forbad them from forming an association and the case appears to have collapsed.

In 1822, the Hawick hosiers attempted to impose another cut in rates. No negotiation was invited and the knitters were forced once again to go on strike. It lasted a gruelling nine months and became famous as The Lang Stand Oot. Only William Beck declined to cut the rates he paid. Cash for the strikers and their hungry families was raised by raffles, concerts and plays as well as through contributions from knitters in Carlisle, Dumfries and Edinburgh who sent what they could spare. The strike succeeded, the employers conceded and Hawick concentrated on producing quality woollen goods – and not only stockings.

All of the skill and marketing experience that had helped the stocking trade to grow eventually led to diversification. In 1828, the Duke of York had his underwear made in Hawick. In an age before central heating and decent insulation, warm underclothes were much prized. Knitting machines were adapted to manufacture sarks or vests and drawers or bloomers as well as what became known later as combinations – the 19th-century equivalent of a onesie. Mechanised spinning jennies or mules powered by water were to turn out a much greater volume of yarn and what would now be recognisable as mills began to open in Hawick, especially on the haughland on the north bank of the Teviot, ground that the town had managed to keep in common ownership. Lades were cut and the water from the river turned several wheels while the fast-flowing Slitrig also drove mills in the centre of the town. Familiar names began to set up in business.

At the same time as Hawick began to industrialise, another utterly distinctive cultural phenomenon appeared. No one who has visited the town or spoken to a Hawick person can fail to have been struck by their remarkable dialect of Scots. Its structure and vocabulary have a great deal in common with the other Border towns but it is the pronunciation of basic words that is very different – 'yow' for you, 'mei' for me, 'sei' for see and many others catch the ear of outsiders. The origins of Hawick's dialect are disputed but it may well be that they are closely linked with the very rapid process of industrialisation that began to accelerate during the Napoleonic wars.

Prompted by the adoption of James Small's swing plough and the consequent reduction in the number of people needed in agriculture, people were leaving the old life on the land. But, when jobs in hosiery in Hawick became available, it appears that within one or two generations, large numbers came to live and work in the town. John Wood, the mapmaker and surveyor, listed the rise in population – in 1801, it was 2,798; in 1811, it rose to 3,688; and it jumped again in 1821 to 4,387. By 1850, more than 11,000 lived in the town and expansion continued. Each time the population jumped, the vast majority of incomers came from the surrounding area and, in any decade between 1841 and 1901 (when census data is available), around 20 per cent of those living in Hawick had arrived relatively recent from the countryside. There were indeed significant groups from both England and Ireland but these were small by comparison, with the latter peaking in the years following the Potato Famine of 1845 to 1852.

According to no less an authority than the great lexicographer, J. A. H. Murray of Denholm, the founder of the Oxford English Dictionary, Hawick's dialect was a version of how country people spoke in Teviotdale in the late 18th and early 19th centuries. He feared it would die out – but he reckoned without the thrawn tenacity of its speakers. And, in essence, what happened was that many former farm workers and their children came at the one time, complete with their country accents, which immediately became a town accent. And it stuck as successive groups arrived to reinforce it. The intensity of mill working and the close sense of community it engendered also helped preserve and develop a very singular mode of speech.

There is, incidentally, a tale that sounds not so much apocryphal as characteristic and it shows that the Hawick dialect extended further east than the boundaries of the town. Recently knighted by Queen Victoria for his pioneering work on the Oxford English Dictionary, homburg-hatted, spade-bearded, wearing a cloak and carrying a silver-topped cane, Sir James Augustus Henry Murray, the son of a Denholm weaver, had come home and was walking across the village green. He was stopped by a stooped old lady who peered up at this commanding figure before saying, 'Mercy mei, Jimsie, is that yow?'

While all of Murray's and others' observations about its origins seem highly plausible, there is another aspect to the dialect that is much harder to understand. Its tone or timbre also seems distinctive. Even without the pronunciation, when Hawick people say see instead of 'sei', their origins are obvious. There was no better example than Bill McLaren. For viewers of international rugby matches, he spoke Scots English and never once said that a tighthead prop had the number 'threi' on his back. But his voice was quintessentially Hawick. But, surprisingly, the distinctive tone is more readily obvious in female voices. It may have been enriched as they struggled to make themselves heard above the racket of machinery in the mills.

In 1824, there was more chatter than ever before in the streets of Hawick because there were more streets. John Wood drew the earliest surviving scale map of the town and noted striking expansion. Along the eastern banks of the Slitrig stood what Wood called the Crescent Quarter, 'a beautiful row of elegant modern houses'. His map also seems to show that Allars Crescent had been built by that time or at least plots laid out. A weir had crossed the Teviot, still clearly visible in the stretch of the river behind Hawick High School, in order to divert water into a mill lade. Wood's map shows it running approximately along the line of Commercial Road before returning to the Teviot where Mansfield Road now stands. Its water powered a string of carding and spinning mills that had been built on the Common Haugh, what Hawick's burgesses had wisely held on to after the legal wrangle with the Dukes of Buccleuch fifty years before. Surprisingly, Wood's map indicates that all the land to the south of the town belonged to the Duke. It did not.

Also marked clearly on Wood's map are a group of mills that had been built on the Common Haugh – what would become the focus of Hawick's industrial area. Roughheugh was the name for the steep bank now more clearly seen rising up behind the car park at Sainsbury's supermarket, and at its foot stood Roughheugh Mill, probably a spinning or carding mill, although Wood does not specify. Near it was Wilton Flour Mill, Langlands Mill, Watson's Spinning Mill and Dickson and Laing's spinning mill. The lade was further branched to turn the wheels of all of these. In 1741, a new bridge had been built across the Teviot to link the town with a road through the Sandbed to the mills on the haugh and Wood's map shows it clearly.

Two other bridges, the Auld and the New, are shown uniting Eastla and Westla, crossing what is called the Slitridge Water. The eastern lade that branched off the Teviot is not included in Wood's map and may therefore postdate 1824. It was dug at Laidlaw's Cauld, opposite the Victoria Laundry, and it supplied power for Laidlaw's Mill. It stood on the site of the B&M Store at the foot of Croft Road.

In all, Wood counted between eight and ten mills carding and spinning local lambswool and he reckoned that half of their output of yarn was made into stockings by the 500 or 600 frames in Hawick and that the other half went for sale in Glasgow. Carpets and blankets were also made and tanning was important – and, surprisingly, in Hawick, not distant. The smell of the faeces (dogs' faeces preferred) and the urine used to tan leather usually meant that this operation lay at some distance, downwind if possible, from housing. But the tannery lay behind the elegant houses of Slitrig Crescent. A third lade is shown coming off the Slitrig to power a 'wool manufactury', the tannery, a flour and a corn mill. Its waters returned to the little river at Tower Dyke Side, under a road bridge.

Elsewhere on Wood's elegantly drawn map there is clear evidence of shifting focus. The ancient route out of the town up Back Raw and through the West Port has been supplanted by the laying out of Buccleuch Street and what is marked as the New Road to Carlisle. The Western Toll has been moved downhill, close to where the High School now stands. And the High Street stretches ever further westwards. In the backlands behind the frontages, buildings seem to have been going up in garden areas and William Beck's stocking shop and his other property are clearly indicated. Each morning and evening townspeople will have walked across to the new mills on the Haugh, and new development to the north of Auld Hawick would be rapid.

Reflecting the recent splits in the Church of Scotland, Wood marked four different churches in Hawick and a Quaker meeting room. In 1824, there was no Catholic chapel – that would come with the Irish in-migrations in mid century. Almost all houses still depended on outside sources of water and wells are marked along most of the main streets. There appear to have been four in the High Street.

Each year, there were four hiring fairs in Hawick, held on quarter days, when farm workers and farmers came into town to negotiate over fees and terms of employment. Common in all the Border market towns, these were in reality little better than slave markets, humiliating for all concerned but especially those men who had been overlooked by the end of the fair day. And that is not a retrospective judgement – farm workers disliked what was a demeaning business as farmers walked up and down, assessing workers, and, at the end of the 20th century, people could still recall the fairs.

Wood also notes a cattle tryst on the third Tuesday of each October. Herds of black cattle had been driven south from the Highlands to the great trysts at Falkirk and Crieff where they were sold to southern buyers. Before the coming of the railways, beasts were driven to slaughter and, as the British Empire expanded, the army and navy were ready markets for salted beef. Until 1777, the drovers had been allowed to rest their herds on Hawick Common but, when this was much reduced, the burgesses withdrew permission. This caused a diversion and, when the herds of black cattle were driven over the hills from Peebles, they came down into the Teviot Valley at Commonside, about seven miles upstream from Hawick before going on to Carlisle. But, in 1785, the drovers petitioned the Hawick burgesses to be allowed to use the common once more and, thinking that an opportunity for business might present itself, they agreed – but only if animals were offered for sale. They probably hoped that local beasts could also be sold on. From Hawick, the herds were driven on to Carlisle or Newcastle. The main drove roads south ran into the Cheviots to Saughtree and then down the North Tyne Valley, or over Mosspaul and down through Ewesdale.

No doubt inspired by all this activity, Andrew Oliver set up his auction business in 1817, holding monthly sales at first in Slitrig Crescent (the owners of 'the elegant modern houses' were probably grateful for the muck for their gardens and a different variety of odour) and then in Bourtree Place. In 1883, Oliver's bought the site where Morrisons supermarket now stands.

As hosiery industrialised and the mill wheels of the carders and spinners turned when the Teviot lades cascaded down them, another logistical problem was solved. Light was vital to all of the textile manufacturing processes, and when a gasworks opened in Hawick in 1830 everyone's lives improved. The strain on workers' sight must have been intense in the long days, often between 5.30 a.m. and 7 p.m. with only two short breaks. But the fitting of gas lamps will have been a boon. The work was hard, repetitive and rarely well paid. But it was less prey to the extravagant slumps and booms of the textile trade in England and part of the reason for that was literature.

Walter Scott and his friend James Hogg draped the shepherds' check over some of their heroes and thereby made the distinctive black and white weave very fashionable. It originated when weavers had first used the natural, undyed fleeces of white and the occasional black sheep to make a simple pattern. But as it grew popular, black dye will have been applied. Trousers were made from the shepherds' check and they became popular in London. That particular fad might have been fleeting if Walter Scott's imagination had not fired a revolution in textile design.

In 1822, King George IV paid a state visit to Edinburgh and Scott was appointed as a kind of stage manager. Following the success of his novels, especially *Waverley* and its setting in the 1745 Jacobite Rising, he clothed the entire event in tartan. The portly king sported a Royal Stewart kilt worn well above the knee over flesh-coloured hose (perhaps made in Hawick) and when the Edinburgh ladies beheld this sight, one was said to remark, 'Since he is here for such a short time, it is as well that we see so much of him.' Despite the pantomime tartanry, with the royal court and their hangers-on sweating through endless reels and strathspeys at Holyroodhouse, the event was a huge success. And it created a market for tartan. Hawick hosiers (making tartan stockings) and tweed makers were busy and the mills of Gala clacked through piles of orders. Whatever the king and the court wore was, in those days, the acme of fashion.

Mythology only lightly disguised as good marketing also helped keep the Border mills busy. The tale runs that John Locke, an expatriate Scot who had visited the towns of Gala and Hawick more than once, received a package from the Dangerfield Mill in Hawick at his tailor's shop in Regent Street in 1847 and he misread the label. Written on the wrapping was the word 'tweel' and, according to myth, Locke wrote back asking for more of this 'tweed'. And so the name of high quality cloth from the Borders was born. This is, of course, nonsense. Locke knew exactly where the Tweed ran and what 'tweel' or twill was. What he very astutely did was invent an excellent brand name that incidentally associated it with the most famous Tweedsider of the times, Sir Walter Scott.

Locke and his dandyish friends were themselves establishing a trend by wearing jackets and trousers of matching fabric. Before they did this, all the emphasis was on the jacket and trousers were often known as 'drabs' and made from black or grey cloth. And, when the Prince of Wales wore a suit of clothes, the trend was set and the mills of Gala and Hawick thrummed on. Royal connections continued and Queen Victoria and Prince Albert's love of the Highlands and all things tartan established an enduring business.

Walter Scott's enormous fame, something with no real modern parallel, also left another legacy. When the railway finally reached Hawick in 1849, the track from Edinburgh was called the Waverley Line and it began at Waverley Station. Not only did it bring tourists to 'Scott Country', it also further charged industry in Hawick. And, when the link to Carlisle was completed in 1862, Hawick had ready access to markets and suppliers from the south and beyond – the British Empire.

Hawick Station stood near where the Teviotdale Leisure Centre is now but what makes its position difficult to visualise is the removal of the embankment to the south that carried the track bed. It is now Mart Street and the viaduct that carried the line over where the roundabout and the entrance to the supermarket car park and petrol station are now has disappeared but the embankment to the south is still clearly visible. The line from Edinburgh into Hawick approached from Hassendean, parallel with the Teviot, and left the town along the banks of the Slitrig.

Striking through the centre, forced by geography to follow the riverbanks, the railway had a profound impact on the urban landscape of Hawick. It changed both the status and value of plots of land and, especially where embankments rose to carry the track bed, it acted as a boundary, creating distinct areas. It may be that there is no such area in the town that could be said to be on the wrong side of the tracks but there are those that are certainly on the other side. To the south, the railway line appeared to restrict outward development, while in the north it marked off the old town from the new terraces and tenements built to house the incoming mill workers. Now that the railway has gone, these ghost boundaries have become less obvious and meaningful, particularly at Mart Street and immediately north of the Teviot where all trace of the station has been swept away. But older folk can still sometimes hear distant whistles and the rhythmic chug of the trains as they pulled away south behind the Town Hall, past the end of Allars Crescent, up the Slitrig, over the viaduct and away into the hills to Carlisle and the world beyond.

Industrial archaeology can be elusive. Often in urban settings, the old is literally obliterated to make room for the new as the future buries the past. But, in Green Lane in Hawick, Buccleuch Mill survives as a silent witness to changing methods of production. At one end of a long rectangular building, a stairwell leads up to two stocking frame flats lit by their characteristic square windows. This part of the mill was built in 1840 but, soon afterwards, a much larger extension was added. The differences are obvious from the outside. The newer part is lit by much larger windows to supply more light for bigger powered machines, broad looms and wider frames.

By comparison with other regions of Britain, the men who worked in the flats at the Buccleuch Mill and elsewhere in Hawick were not badly paid. According to a survey of 1845, frame knitters in the Borders could earn up to 50 per cent more than their fellow workers in England, in areas such as West Yorkshire and Nottinghamshire. There were two main reasons for this disparity. In the Borders, the population was significantly lower and skilled labour relatively scarce. And the business was structured differently. Those men who made stockings for Bailie John Hardie were paid directly by him and he took orders directly from customers. In West Yorkshire and elsewhere in England, middlemen often bought stockings from knitters before selling them on at a profit to retailers. Their cut inevitably took money out of the pockets of the frame workers.

In the 1840s, English knitters began to migrate in numbers to Hawick. A recent analysis of census data has shown up this trend very clearly. In 1841, the enumerators asked respondents for their places of birth and, in Hawick, a large proportion, 25 per cent, were recent immigrants and many of these had come north from Yorkshire and Nottinghamshire. At 4 per cent of the town's population, more than 400 people, these English incomers and their accents will have been very noticeable in the shops and pubs of the High Street and their expertise very welcome in the mills and workshops. This percentage remained steady until the end of the 19th century. Hawick has a clear and important English heritage. But apart from their knitting skills and their DNA, the immigrants brought something else from the south.

Victorian Britain was beginning to develop a near obsession with mass sport. Before work was organised into factories and mills and hours became gradually regulated by law, exertion for the sake of it was not something exhausted manual workers sought. Rest mattered much more. But as the five-and-a-half-day week became more common, so did surplus time and energy. Cricket was tremendously popular down south and English soldiers were the first to introduce it to Scotland. Kelso is one of the oldest clubs, with records stretching back to the 1820s. Twenty years later, immigrant textile workers from Yorkshire in particular brought cricket to Hawick and the names of good players have survived. Val Godfrey, Thomas Esplin, the brothers Henry and Alfred Hunt and John and Harry Turvill all played alongside home-grown talent in the shape of Jim Fiddes and Dandy Henderson.

In 1849, there were three teams in the town – Hawick, Western Star and Wilton all played against each other on the Haugh. If other teams, such as Kelso, came to play, records have not survived. By 1860, Hawick had amalgamated with Wilton and the Duke of Buccleuch gave the use of Buccleuch Park as a dedicated cricket ground. The club has remained there ever since. In the same year, Hawick and Wilton played their first recorded fixture against Langholm and, as the railway began to make travel faster and easier between the Border towns, a summer fixture list grew. In 2010, the club celebrated 150 happy years at Buccleuch Park.

As sport became more popular, breeches were going out of fashion. With the spread of railway transport and the move of the mass of people off the land and into the industrialising cities and towns, fewer people wore hose or rode horses and more and more men favoured trousers. This provided a temporary problem for Hawick hosiery but the stocking makers quickly adapted. Instead, they began to make woollen underwear, an itchy thought, but nevertheless a change in output that proved very successful indeed. Vests, pants, combinations and what were known as cholera belts (these unlikely garments were made popular by British soldiers in India who believed it was possible to ward off cholera by wearing a kind of cummerbund to keep the midriff and the vital organs warm – and in Victorian Britain it was thought generally good to wrap a wide belt around as a preventative measure for all sorts of ailments) all needed wider frames.

This diversification prompted a move by some mill owners to

steam-driven broad frames and the first of these were introduced to Hawick by John Laing and Son in 1858. The new machinery was operated and maintained by an English foreman, James Bonsor. The introduction of steam changed the townscape radically and early panoramic photographs show a dozen or so tall mill lums punctuating the skyline. The last survivor is the magnificent redbrick lum behind Peter Scott's in Buccleuch Street. This change in process was made possible by the ability of the railway to bring coal in bulk to Hawick and mill owners were encouraged to change over by the chancy nature of water power. Dry summers could reduce the power of the flow through the lades considerably. Nevertheless, the switchover to steam was by no means universal.

One of Hawick's most impressive buildings is Tower Mill. A stunning feat of engineering, the whole structure of this carding and spinning mill is balanced on a single-span bridge over the Slitrig. It opened in 1850, the property of William Elliot & Sons, and its 14-foot undershot wheel turned for the first time. And it kept turning. From the early 20th century, the Tower Mill wheel was used to generate electricity. The building has now been beautifully converted into a cinema and arts centre and the great wheel is still there, visible under a glass floor.

After the 1850s, textile manufacturing began to move more and more into mills and the number of small-scale stocking shops slowly declined as Hawick once again expanded. The Ordnance Survey of 1858 supplies a fascinating snapshot. For example, the wonderfully detailed map shows for the first time the full extent of the lading on the Slitrig. Cut into the bank below Whitlaw Wood, a channel branched off to power the wheels of Lynwood Mill, what looks to have been the largest complex of mill buildings in Hawick at that time, at least according to the scale. It had its own gasometer and, indeed, its own lade. The cut returned water to the Slitrig as the little river rounded the bend at Lynwood to flow almost due north.

The Ordnance Survey shows the centre of Hawick much more

densely built up but there is also a series of large new houses, schools and churches on the outskirts. A church, a big manse and two short streets of housing meeting at a corner have been built at Myreslaw Green and a ribbon of development has extended much further up the Loan towards Crumhaugh Hill. Opposite the mouth of the Slitrig, on the north bank of the Teviot, a large gasworks is shown, built to supply the mills on the Haugh. And the Sandbed and the area between the Teviot and the High Street, as far as the old East Port, have been densely built up with most of the backland area used for housing or other buildings. Behind the building now marked as the Tower Hotel, Allars Crescent and its tenements have been clearly completed and more housing for mill workers was built on the streets to the south-east that lead off the High Street. And a new cemetery to provide a different sort of accommodation has been dug off Wellogate Brae. For the first time, the map draws the line of the burgh of barony and Hawick is already bursting through it. At the time of the Ordnance Survey of 1858, the population stood at just over 12,000.

In 1866, John Rutherfurd wrote a well-judged description of the town for *The Southern Counties Register and Directory*:

> Probably no provincial town in Scotland has undergone such a change in appearance and limits as Hawick of late years. It has extended its bounds on all sides, while internally, the new erections which have replaced the previous thatched and mean-looking houses, have so transformed and renovated the ancient burgh as to give it much of a metropolitan aspect. The new banks and shops would be a credit to the principal streets of any city, while the well-kept streets themselves possess a bustle never seen but in large commercial markets.

On 12 April 1861, Confederate troops fired on Fort Sumter in South Carolina. The American Civil War had begun. It was immensely bitter and destructive with more than a quarter of a million dead on both sides before General Robert E. Lee was forced to surrender in June 1865. The South believed that cotton would win the war. Because the Western European economies were so dependant on Confederate cotton for their textile industries, Jefferson Davis and his generals were certain that Britain and France would be compelled to support them against the Union armies. But President Lincoln immediately instigated what was a very effective naval blockade of the Southern ports. The export of cotton to Europe had ground to a complete halt by 1862. And, once again, wars in foreign fields were to prove very beneficial to Hawick.

What became known as 'the cotton famine' starved the Lancashire mills in particular of their essential raw material and new markets for woollen textiles began to open up straightaway. Hawick vests, pants, cholera belts and combinations were all made from lambswool. Much of it was locally sourced so supply was unaffected by events abroad. In addition to the warmth it gave wearers, Hawick underwear was marketed as unshrinkable – a very important quality given how often it needed to be washed. And colour was of no importance in a society where what was worn beneath outerwear was very rarely seen by anyone other than the owner. In addition to the cotton famine, another moment of serendipity triggered Hawick's expansion. The winters of 1864 to 1867 were very severe. In 1866, an unprecedented 2.5-metre snowdrift piled up in London's Regent Street and, in Aberdeen a year later, there were 6-metre snowdrifts. As the snow fell, the mills hummed with orders for cosy combinations, vests and bloomers and sales boomed.

In Langholm, change of another sort was stirring – something else that would define modern Hawick. William Webb Ellis may have picked up a football and run with it at Rugby School in 1823 but he did not invent rugby in a blinding flash of inspiration, 'with a fine disregard for the rules'. The point was that there were no rules. What happened after that date was the codification of the rules of the game and its adaptation into something manageable – a game that could be played regularly and relatively safely by groups of young boys. Instead of vast, unlimited teams playing on a pitch a mile wide, as at Carterhaugh, for most of a day, a version of handba quickly evolved that was shorter, safer and involved smaller numbers. Rules for what became known as rugby football, that is, the version of football played at Rugby and other schools like it, were produced in 1845. At that time, the Football Association included clubs that played different sorts of football but, when Blackheath in London broke away in 1863, the two games quickly grew apart. The Rugby Football Union was formed in 1871 and the game came to the Borders in the same year.

A match was advertised in Langholm for 31 December 1871, by three young men. William Scott, Alfred Moses and William Lightbody had all been educated at English public schools like Rugby and had learned to play that version of the game. But so many turned up on the 31st of December that Scott simply divided the crowd into two teams and marked out a pitch. The score was not recorded.

At the end of the following summer, Hawick and Wilton Cricket Club bought a ball – not a cricket ball but a football. Their members wanted to keep fit over the winter and they thought for a moment or two about playing football. But the Rugby version was preferred since it was 'manlier and more congenial to the Border nature than the tamer association game'. Exactly. And in 1873, the opposition turned up. A fixture was set between Hawick and Langholm but, before play could begin, all 40 players had to agree on the rules. What was to be the definition of a goal or converted try? Was it the kicking of the ball over or under the crossbar? Against Carlisle in a previous fixture, Langholm had agreed that a goal was scored when the ball was kicked between the posts but under the crossbar. Which was ironic. The game at Hawick was declared a draw because their goal kicker sent his conversion over the bar. Oh dear.

At first, Hawick played in blue and white striped jerseys, navy shorts (probably much longer than the modern style), blue and white striped stockings and many players wore caps. Those still awarded to international players are a memory of that habit. How they kept them on in the depths of a scrummage is a mystery. In 1885, the club was reconstituted as Hawick Football Club. There was no mention of 'Rugby' and this was not unusual. The Scottish Football Union did not add the word 'Rugby' to its name until 1924, when Murrayfield opened. New colours were adopted – the famous dark green jerseys and stockings with white shorts. Some believe that, when the crowd shout 'Hawway the Robbie Dyes', they are remembering the man who mixed that colour but apparently Robbie Dye was a particularly fanatical supporter. In 1886, Hawick was admitted to the Scottish Football Union. Two years later, the club moved to the other end of the town to Mansfield Park. And, in 1896, they won the first of many Scottish championship titles.

Despite the consistent quality of Borders rugby and the fact that the region was, for a century, the heartland of the game in Scotland, the Scottish Rugby Union was long dominated by the former pupils clubs of the fee-paying schools of Edinburgh and Glasgow. Between 1871 and 1914, 118 international matches were played between Scotland and other nations and yet only 11 Borderers were selected to turn out for their country in that period of 43 years. These attitudes persisted for a long time and players from the FP clubs or London Scottish were usually preferred over Borders players until the 1960s.

Resentments simmered early. At a meeting of the Border clubs in St Boswells to discuss 'the great dissatisfaction which exists in the South with the present state of matters, and the best way to secure redress of grievances and the furtherance of rugby would be easier promoted through the formation of a South of Scotland Rugby Union'. Nothing came of this immediately but the unhappiness of the clubs finally expressed itself in the creation of the Border League in 1901 – despite the lofty disapproval of the Scottish Rugby Union. Hawick, Langholm, Jedforest, Melrose and Gala combined to form the first competitive rugby league in the world.

It was Rugby League that lay at the heart of the Scottish Rugby

Union's antipathy. The FP clubs in Edinburgh and Glasgow had seen the formation of what eventually became known as the Rugby League in 1895 after disagreements over payments to working men who took time off to play. Many northern clubs turned professional and some talented Borderers were tempted south to become professionals. Run by men who mostly held middle-class jobs in the cities, the Scottish Rugby Union was anxious about the Border League becoming the Border Rugby League and joining the clubs of Northern England. Distances were after all not extreme, railways ran and, because of the textile industry, there existed many personal links between the likes of Huddersfield and Hawick. And so the SRU cracked down as hard as they could and those players from Borders clubs who had turned professional were excluded for life as many came back home after retirement. Now half-forgotten in the new era of professional rugby union, this was a disgraceful disfigurement to the game. Several Hawick players who had given great service as amateurs were not even allowed to come as spectators to Mansfield Park after they had left clubs such as Workington, St Helens or Leeds.

Between 1863 and 1899, the Hawick economy surged ahead. The manufacture of woollen underwear began to concentrate in the mills of larger companies, some of them names now familiar. They developed brands customers could recognise and ask for in shops – Lyle and Scott made Ellaness vests, pants and other items, Peter Scott created Pesco goods and Innes Henderson (later Braemar) had Henderwick underwear. The population of the town rocketed, almost doubling from 12,000 in 1863 to nearly 20,000 by the end of the century. Not only did the railway reach Carlisle in 1862 and place Hawick securely on a worldwide communications network, the fabric of the town began to fill out as it acquired familiar architecture and modern institutions. The *Hawick Advertiser* was founded in 1854 and the venerable Hawick Archaeological Society, a true adornment, met for the first time in 1856. On a less elevated level, a new sewage system was dug in 1877 to service the expanding town and include all of the new housing and mills on the Wilton side of the Teviot and east of the station towards Mansfield. In 1861, the Burgh Improvement Act had united Hawick and Wilton parishes into one civic entity. In the second half of the 19th century, six new schools were built and, helped by funding from the Scots-American philanthropist, Andrew Carnegie, a superb library was built beside the new bridge (completed in 1832) over the Teviot to service Hawick Station. The excellent Hawick Cooperative Society opened its doors for business in 1885 and, the year before, the status of the town was much enhanced by the opening of a new town hall – the present building that towers above the High Street and still plays a central role.

The look of late Victorian Hawick owes an enormous debt to one man, a tremendously talented and inventive architect. J. P. Alison was versatile, able to create buildings to suit the varied tastes of his many clients; he was fluent in Palladian, Gothic, Mock Tudor, Art Nouveau, Dutch genres and Arts and Crafts styles of building. Born in Eskbank in 1862, James Pearson Alison moved to set up in business in Hawick where he had relatives. After opening an office in 1888, he began to attract commissions almost immediately. The textile business was booming, the mills were thrumming and those who enjoyed their profits had money to spend.

Alison had many buildings raised in Hawick and one of the most successful is no. 1 North Bridge Street – what was the Central Hotel. It finishes the eastern vista along the High Street as Bourtree Place and North Bridge Street divide. Its elegant balustrade above the big bay window and the outshot pavement frontage used to carry letters spelling 'The Central Hotel'. They are clearly visible in early photographs. The hotel was run by a colourful, self-assured proprietor, George Luff. A native of Brighton, he involved himself in Hawick society with gusto. When he placed an advertisement in *The Hawick News* in February 1888 for a meeting of his Masonic Lodge, he did not hide his light: 'Masonic Lodge 424 will be expected to turn out well on Tuesday first. The fearless, energetic secretary, Bro. Luff, will be present.' That sort of confidence, swagger even, typified the dynamism that seemed to permeate the late Victorian town. For some reason, Luff's old Central Hotel building was said to be at the 'Coffin End of the High Street'. This was a reference, still current, to a line of single storey shops that stretched out from the site of what would become the Central Hotel to beyond the place where the Horse (see p. 152) used to stand. The hotel closed in 1919 and the lettering on the balustrade was changed to read 'Prudential'. The insurance company had offices in the buildings until the mid 1950s.

Further down North Bridge is a terrace of beautiful red sandstone townhouses designed by J. P. Alison. Numbers 41 to 49 fluently combine elements of Arts and Crafts, Art Nouveau and Dutch styling in the gables – a detail the architect was fond of. Alison's home and office were at no. 45, and on the doorstep his monogram can still be seen, picked out in mosaic tiling. In 1894, the same year as the Central Hotel opened, a rival of sorts in the shape of the Liberal Club was completed at the corner of the High Street and Brougham Place. Perhaps one of Alison's less successful buildings with a mix of features that fail to cohere, it, nevertheless, plants itself stolidly on a difficult, sloping corner site. For political balance, he also designed the Conservative Club in nearby Bourtree Place. More Palladian and, well, conservative in style, it still impresses. One of its neighbours, the Congregational Church, shows yet more of Alison's versatility. A Gothic creation, again on an awkward, sloping corner site, its interior is beautifully realised. And, to complete a sense of the remarkable range of J. P. Alison, a building at the opposite end of Hawick stands in very pleasing contrast to the stateliness of his work around the east end of the High Street. The Hawick Bowling Club Pavilion is built in a playful mock-Tudor style, its half-timbering somehow appropriate to the ancient game of bowls played on the immaculate lawn. It was also the scene of William Irvine's triumph in the Pow Cup before the First World War.

Alison was not only hugely prolific, he was also thoughtful, constantly considering what would work best for a client and the chosen site. In 1902, he designed a beautifully delicate shop front and interior fittings for a baker's shop at 16–18 High Street. Thomas Brydon and Sons' windows and ingo doorway are masterly – something Charles Rennie Mackintosh would not have been unhappy to put off his hands.

Money was being made by mill owners by the end of the 19th century and J. P. Alison was commissioned to build some grand houses. Woodnorton in Sunnyhill Road was completed in 1908 (as Craigmore) for Robert Pringle, the grandson of the founder of Pringle of Scotland. With characteristic crow-stepped gables, it was built in a Scottish Renaissance style with a fine square tower over the main entrance and a ballroom extension to the rear. But perhaps the most attractive of the big hooses for the mill-owning families is Norwood in Roadhead. It was commissioned by Peter Scott in 1903. A variant of the Arts and Crafts style, it manages to be both substantial and homely. With its pillared arches and wood panelling, the entrance hall is a wonderfully well-conceived space and the main drawing room is flooded with light. Upstairs the main bedroom has French windows that give on to a balcony and a sweeping view. At the rear of the house is a superbly modelled little porch with white pillars. Fashion shows were held on the lawns of Norwood and the Scott family owned this stunning house until 1964.

The architecture of Hawick is the sum of many designs, talents and accidents of geography but J. P. Alison's work is remarkable in its quality and versatility. Each one of his buildings is worth stopping to look at. Deservedly, he was successful and, reputedly, one of the first in Hawick to own a motor car. A member of the Hawick Archaeological Society, the Hawick Callants Club and a Fellow of the Society of Antiquaries of Scotland, he made an immense contribution to the town – one that should be more celebrated. His firm survives as Aitken Turnbull Architects but perhaps the only stain on Alison's wonderful legacy is the sad fact that they are based in Gala.

In the second half of the 19th century, Hawick Common Riding acquired its decidedly Victorian look – one that it shares with the other older festivals at Selkirk and Langholm. Top hats, tailcoats, rosettes and much of the structure of the annual celebration as it is now were all put in place in the wake of crisis. As ex-Provost J. C. G. Landles wrote in the *Transactions of the Hawick Archaeological Society* of 1951:

> There have been times when the festival has sunk to a very low standard, when the Ceremonial aspect was almost completely submerged by the celebration aspect. So serious had the position become about three quarters of a century ago that the Council had practically washed their hands of the whole business. There were still those in the town, however, who had a deep regard for our ancient ceremonies. A few of these gentlemen, whose names are known and revered today as those of worthy townsmen, got together and persuaded the Provost of the time [Provost Watson] to make an attempt to have the position rectified. The attempt was successful, a new Ceremonial Committee was formed and a new start on the lines laid down by that Committee and I think I am safe in saying that from that day, the Common-Riding has never looked back. The ceremonies are discharged with due regard to ancient records. The Cornets carry the burden of office with seriousness and dignity, and the celebration never goes beyond the bounds of good taste.

Or at least not often. Landles was referring to the reluctance of the Town Council to take responsibility for the Common Riding. In 1857, they had refused to discharge their traditional obligation to elect a Cornet and, therefore, endorse him and the celebrations. Apparently the merriment had been getting out of hand. A furious petition persuaded councillors to change their minds but reform had been entered on the agenda. And it seems to have been needed. In 1868, a little boy called George Marriot ran out in front of the mounted cavalcade in the town and was killed and, in 1876, Edward Deardon was fatally injured when a horse bolted into the crowd. The Cornet and some of his supporters were arrested on charges of reckless riding, but they were later released. But there were improvements elsewhere and, by 1885, the Town Council had agreed to back the Common Riding and, two years later, the Ceremonial Committee noted by ex-Provost Landles had been set up to administer the celebrations. In the same year, the Kirkin of the Cornet was introduced and a Cornet's Chaplain appointed. It was all becoming more respectable, perhaps even more sober. The structure, schedule and the nature of the ceremonies were essentially fixed in the 1890s and these have changed little since then.

In the late 19th century, cashmere was first seen in Hawick. Derived from the place name of Kashmir, the wool of goats from India, Afghanistan, Iran, Mongolia and elsewhere had originally been seen in Britain as an informal import from the Raj and cashmere yarn had been spun in Glasgow since the 1830s. The problem was the separation of the coarser fibre known as guard hair, the outer coat of the goat, from the much softer undercoat of these creatures that lived in cold and windy climates. It was this double coat that kept them warm and dry. Dawson International claim to have been the inventors of a de-hairing machine in the 1890s and, after that time, scarves and jumpers appear to have been made in small quantities in Hawick. An unintended consequence of the increasing import of cashmere was that this dense fibre carried seeds in it. As the wool was washed, these floated down the Teviot and took root as the giant hogweed and Himalayan balsam plants. The hogweed in particular threatened to choke and destroy the native flora of the riverbanks with stands of 12 feet in places but a successful programme of eradication was completed under the auspices of Tweed Forum by 2007.

Cashmere products were one of the early signals of a move towards the manufacture of outerwear as well as underwear. Hawick producers began to experiment with versions of Fair Isle and Shetland jumpers and to diversify into what were known as gents' cardigans. In 1905,

Innes Henderson was knitting jumpers in some volume. When World War One was declared in 1914, both underwear and warm outerwear were wanted by the armed forces and, once again, conflict brought business to the town. In the damp winter trenches, jumpers were necessary and, when new recruits were issued with underwear, it was the first time many of them had worn any. Those who survived the slaughter of the Somme and the other bloody battles would continue to wear it and, for all the wrong reasons, they became a new market for what was made in Hawick.

The Ordnance Survey of 1899 is fascinating. In that year, the population of Hawick soared to almost 20,000 – its highest-ever level – although the map does not yet include the large peripheral housing estates at Burnfoot, Silverbuthall, Stirches, Crumhaugh and Weensland. All of those would be built in the later 20th century. That must have meant a tremendous density of accommodation in the centre of Hawick, in the tenements of the streets leading off the High Street in particular. There is one other poignant feature and that is the creation of Drumlanrig Square. It involved the demolition of Auld Mid Raw, the disappearance of the last vestige of the old Anglian village between the two rivers. Mills have been built all over the new map of Hawick and, by 1914, a small number of large companies had come to dominate the industrial landscape of the town.

8

HAWICK LOST AND FOUND

In 1914, the guns of August roared. Seven German armies rumbled into Belgium, reduced the defences of Liège and Namur to rubble, and having crossed the French frontier, they dashed to seize Paris. Halted by desperate sacrifice at the Battle of the Marne, the Germans were soon forced to entrench and a meandering string of labyrinthine trench works quickly built up along a line from the North Sea coast to the Swiss borders. For four years of appalling, relentless slaughter, it moved very little and what became known as the Western Front was the major battleground of the First World War.

Hawick men died there in their hundreds and the cemeteries of Flanders are hollow with their graves. From the records of the Commonwealth War Graves Commission and of local newspapers, 693 names are entered on the town's Roll of Honour but its compilers confess that even these staggering numbers may be an underestimate. Recent research has arrived at a death toll of close to a thousand from the town and the area around. Statistics, even lists of names, can numb sensibilities but, if the doleful roll of the Hawick dead is read in detail, an even more staggering picture comes slowly into focus.

No source is definitive but it is generally believed that about a million men from Great Britain and Northern Ireland died in the First World War – about 4 per cent of the male population. In Hawick, the numbers are almost double – close to 8 per cent – and, if the estimate of a thousand is accepted, it climbs to a shocking 11 per cent. And the impact in a small town of such unrelenting, wholesale carnage over a relatively short period was much greater. If many more than 700 young men lost their lives in four brutal years of conflict, their deaths were felt in virtually every street and by most extended families. The detail drives home how badly Hawick was hit.

Three sets of three brothers were killed. George, James and Tom Douglas of 6 Wilton Hill Terrace did not return home. Tom died on 15 April 1917, George on 20 November 1917 and, in what must have seemed to their parents and family a shatteringly cruel twist of fate, James was killed on 17 October 1918, only three weeks before the armistice and the suspension of hostilities. A month before, James Montgomery of Wilton Hill was killed. His brother William had died in November 1914 and their brother, George, in 1917. The Porter brothers of 3 Rinkvale Cottages were all reported dead in 1917 and 1918. Relatives were informed by War Office telegram and it is difficult to imagine the agony of mothers and fathers as these were handed over on Hawick doorsteps by postmen who knew exactly what the news was. It is hard to comprehend the impact of one death but how families dealt with the death of twenty-five sets of two brothers from Hawick is beyond understanding. They carried familiar names like Scott, Storie, Cranston, Nichol, McLeod, Douglas and Brydon.

Turkey was allied to Germany and Austria and an amphibious assault on the heights of Gallipoli, not far from the capital of Istanbul, occupies a sad, dark corner of Hawick's history. In a badly planned, near-suicidal series of landings that were repelled by solid Turkish defences, it is believed that no fewer than eighty young men from the town were killed.

Almost every week telegrams bearing tragic news were delivered to addresses all over Hawick and sometimes the losses were very concentrated. Near neighbours grieved with each other as news of their boys' deaths came from France – eleven young men did not walk up Gladstone Street again and eleven more who had enlisted never came back to Allars Crescent.

A hundred years after the outbreak of hostilities, there is no one now in the Borders who remembers how the First World War affected those left behind in Hawick or the Borders. But in 1999, an interview was recorded with Jennie Corbett of Selkirk and she recalled in sharp detail the experiences of women and families in those tragic years.

It was a wee while before news of the first casualties came through. There was no wireless, no one had the phone and you used to get it by what we called Reuters. These messages were sent and we were sent at dinnertime to read the notice boards and report to the school where the teachers used to shift these wee flags on a great big map.

There was a postman stayed next door to us, and I mind him saying to my mother one day, 'Ee ken, Mrs Beattie, I used to like my job, but no' now. As soon as I get one of those buff envelopes [a War Office telegram] into my hand, I say to myself that's a sair heart for somebody.'

They got a little buff envelope to say that somebody was killed in action, missing or wounded. That was all. If they were missing, they might turn up, if they were wounded then somebody would surely write. They could go a long time without any [further] correspondence, no nothing, just the worry.

An awful lot of women were back at the mills at that time, doing men's jobs. And when I was a pirn winder I was sent up to Bridgehaugh Mill [in Selkirk] and it was all married women who were there. They were all soldiers' wives or mothers. And they used to send Belle Brown and me to their different houses in the morning, after the post had been. You were always feared that some woman's mother would give you a buff letter. Sometimes their mothers (who were looking after the house and the bairns) would look hard at you and say, 'Tell her the post's not been yet.' If anyone got bad news, it was bad news for everybody because in the first part of the war, it was the local battalions that were all together, just laddies.

The Roll of Honour for Hawick and the War Memorial list the names of the dead, the muster of an army of lost boys, those who could only walk the ghost road home. Even at the distance of a century or so, it is difficult to suppress anger at the waste, the tears and the hollowing pain of all that needless loss.

Four years before the thunder of the guns stilled, in what will have seemed to Hawick men in the mud and squalor of the trenches like another world, the town had celebrated its quatercentenary. A Grand Historical Pageant paraded around the Volunteer Park. It was led by a young woman sitting demurely in a shell-shaped carriage. She was Miss Margot Barclay and her dress and crown proclaimed her as The Queen of the Borderland or, more directly, in the words of one of the best fragments of poetry about the town, 'Hawick's Queen o' a' the Border'. Her carriage was gently drawn by twenty-one pages – bewigged boys wearing white Regency costume, appropriately complete with breeches and hose. At least two of these somewhat bewildered laddies were to lose their big brothers in Flanders. The pageant was trumpeted by a fanfare and announced by a group of heralds. In less than a year, two of them had died on the Western Front.

The central event of the quatercentenary and its most enduring legacy was the memory of the consequences of another military disaster. On Thursday, 4 June 1914, Lady Sybil Scott unveiled the splendid bronze sculpture known to generations since simply as the Horse. To commemorate the triumphant return from Hornshole, it was made by William Beattie, a native of Hawick, and it is a superb achievement. Only a month before the armistice of 1918, Beattie was killed in action.

Most of those men who never came back knew Stobs Camp, a huge and half-forgotten army base on the banks of the Slitrig to the south of the town. Bought by the War Office from the Elliot family in 1902, it grew quickly to accommodate almost 20,000 men at its peak. At 4,000 acres, the Stobs estate was large enough to allow manoeuvres, there was a rifle range and space for cavalry training.

Serviced by the Waverley Line, it had its own dedicated railway station. In the wake of the Battle of the Marne in 1914, Stobs was converted into a prisoner of war camp for thousands of captured German and Austrian soldiers, 6,000 in all. It had been a landscape of conical white tents, used mainly in the summer months, but when the first prisoners arrived by train in November 1914, it was decided that they should be accommodated in more than 200 asbestos and corrugated iron huts. Quickly prefabricated and erected by Hawick tradesmen, they supplied substantial work for local businesses. Stobs Camp was also used in the Second World War, principally as a resettlement camp for soldiers from the Free Polish Army, and it was finally closed in 1959. Little remains of it.

Stobs had a surprising and positive legacy. When the War Office first purchased the estate from the Elliot family in 1902, the scale of what was planned understandably caused concern in Hawick. Quickly dubbed 'Scotland's Aldershot', the camp's 20,000 soldiers could easily have swamped the life of the town, changing it radically. To ensure the preservation of local traditions and to foster local art and literature, the Hawick Callants Club was founded in 1904. For more than a century, it has fulfilled its original aims to a remarkable degree, not only publishing and updating Hawick's song and poetry but also bringing its history closer with the erection and emplacement of a series of plaques at important sites around the town.

Private James Guthrie of the King's Own Scottish Borderers survived the Great War but only for another twenty years. Wounded in the disastrous assault on Gallipoli in Turkey, he recovered and eventually transferred to the Royal Signals as a motorcycle dispatch rider. It was at that moment he discovered a passion – and a talent – for motorbikes. After returning to Hawick in 1919, he bought an army surplus machine and soon afterwards was involved in an accident at Howdenburn. On his appearance at the Sheriff Court Jimmie was admonished with the warning from the bench that 15 mph was dangerously fast for that corner.

The Hawick Motorcycle Club was very active and Guthrie quickly began to rise through the placings at races in the countryside around the town. These were usually hill climbs or flat races on grass tracks. No motorbike events were run on tarmac in Scotland until after the Second World War when redundant airfields were commandeered. The Hawick club realised that they had a star in the making and sponsored Jimmie's first entry in the famous Isle of Man TT races. His bike broke down on the second lap.

Undeterred, the Hawick rider practised and improved. Races were also run on sand tracks and the richest and most prestigious in the North of England was held at Druridge Bay on the Northumberland coast. Crowds of around 30,000 watched riders race around fifteen laps. Jimmie won the Open in 1926 and the prize of fifty guineas, as well as the 350cc race. And a month later, on the straight line of the West Sands at St Andrews, he won the Scottish Speed Championships.

New Hudson Motorcycles of Birmingham offered Jimmie a works bike, a specially tuned machine, to compete in the 1927 Isle of Man TT. He accepted and, when the race began, telegrams were sent every few minutes to Hawick to update the townsfolk on the progress of the race. Jimmie and his brother Archie had opened a garage at 61 High Street and the telegrams were posted every few minutes on the windows for the crowd that had gathered outside. He came second. With his brother Archie tuning his bike, Jimmie practised hard around Hawick. The A7 to the north of the town was thought to have stretches similar to the roads on the Isle of Man. Teindside Bridge and Ancrum Bridge also resembled bridges on the TT course.

When Jimmie switched to riding AJS bikes, he was immediately successful, winning the TT lightweight race in 1930. He began to compete on the European Grand Prix circuit, doing well in Holland and Germany. A redesign of the Norton bike persuaded another change, one that was to prove crucial. Between 1931 and 1937, Jimmie won twenty-six TT and Grand Prix races. His riding style was much admired. Crouching flat and forward across the petrol tank to minimise wind resistance, he also maintained as high a gear as possible throughout a race, concentrating completely on the track, leaning expertly around its twists and turns.

In August 1937, the Norton team arrived at the Sachsenring Circuit for the German Grand Prix. Watched by 250,000 spectators, it was the premiere European motorcycle event in the calendar and, with the success of the BMW team, expectations were high. At forty, Jimmie Guthrie was the oldest competitor but nevertheless he led by some distance with a lap to go. The Union Jack was ready at the finish line. But the Hawick rider never appeared. For some unknown reason, under no pressure and with the race virtually won, Guthrie's bike left the road and finished in a ditch amongst a stand of saplings. He sustained terrible injuries and died soon afterwards in hospital. It may be that his bike seized and he lost control but there have been suggestions of foul play. Whatever the cause, one of Hawick's very greatest sporting heroes was dead – but he is not forgotten.

Guthrie also left a more tangible legacy than a memorial. Steve Hislop from Chesters was a phenomenally successful racer, winning no fewer than eleven Isle of Man TT titles as well as having tremendous success with superbikes. And, like Jimmie Guthrie, he died young – but not on the track. On 30 July 2003, he was on board a helicopter that crashed near Teviothead. A memorial cairn was raised to Steve Hislop, known as Hizzy, by his many devoted supporters.

Into the Valley of Death rode the six hundred on 25 October 1854. And into legend. And knitwear. Despite the fact that the Charge of the Light Brigade came about through farcical aristocratic military incompetence and enmity, the crazy image of British cavalry wielding sabres and lances charging a well-organised battery of Russian guns became famous as an example of reckless courage and an uncompromising devotion to following orders in the service of the British Empire – even if those orders were suicidally stupid. Perhaps the most positive outcome was that the Charge of the Light Brigade eventually helped stimulate the Hawick knitwear industry.

The charge was led by James Brudenell, the 7th Earl of Cardigan, at the Battle of Balaclava in the Crimean War. Conditions were so cold on the northern shores of the Black Sea that not only was the balaclava invented but the cardigan was also adopted. Named after the reckless earl, it was originally a knitted waistcoat worn under a jacket. Having acquired sleeves, it became popular on the back of the fame of the charge, particularly when it was immortalised by Alfred, Lord Tennyson's deeply daft but irritatingly stirring poem.

Cardigans had been produced in Hawick for the equally chill conditions in the trenches of the First World War and they continued to be popular after the armistice. As did underwear. Between 1919 and 1939, when the shadows of war darkened Europe once more, outerwear and underwear were equivalent in volume in Hawick as firms carried on making both. As the textile industry slowly pulled out of the post-war depression (until 1922–23 business was poor and many mills worked on short time), fashions began to change. Women appropriated the gents' cardigan as they gave up the traditional pre-war white blouse for something warmer and more colourful. In 1922 Innes Henderson (later Braemar) advertised a very varied product range that included men's jackets, waistcoats, jerseys and cardigans (listed as 'coat sweaters') as well as ladies' sports coats, jumpers and children's woollens. And, at the same time, the mill turned out the Kumfy range of underwear, including the ever-popular cholera belts.

In 1934, the manufacture of outerwear in Hawick changed significantly with the arrival of a talented and charismatic individual. Appointed as a designer by Robert Pringle & Son, Otto Weisz came from Austria and he changed the look and the prospects for Hawick knitwear radically. Up until 1934, ladies' and gents' jumpers had been of a standard shape with a round neck and a limited range of colours. And the mills had relied on senior production staff to make decisions about how their garments looked. Weisz came up with the hugely popular twinset – a ladies' cardigan with a short-sleeved jumper of the same colour worn under it. These were an enormous and immediate success. Not only did he alter the cut and offer a wide range of attractive pastel colours, he also created new necklines and cuff-lines. They were knitted from a variety of yarns but the Austrian understood clearly how colour and texture interacted. Using only the under-fleece of the cashmere goats, Weisz enabled the use of soft and subtle dyes. Pringle's success created a virtuous circle in Hawick because it forced other mills to take on designers to compete in an expanding market.

Before creating the twinset, Pringles had used the famous Argyle pattern in its fabrics. Made popular by the then Prince of Wales (a keen but inexpert golfer), it was adapted from the tartan of Clan Campbell, whose heartland is in Argyll. So-called tartan hose were knitted in the pattern but jumpers came to be made with the characteristic lozenge-shape and in strong colours. The link with golf persisted, especially when Pringle made the excellent decision to sponsor Arnold Palmer and Gary Player in the 1960s and Nick Faldo and Colin Montgomerie in the 1980s, and the pattern is still the most recognisable sign of a jumper made by the former Hawick company. Since 2000 production has ceased in Hawick and is now carried on in Asia although some finishing used to be done in the town so that a 'Made in Scotland' label could be attached. Now Pringle only has an office in Hawick – a sad end to a great success story.

Pringles had long understood and exploited celebrity endorsement and, immediately after the Second World War, it came from Hollywood. In 1949, the Scottish-born actress, Deborah Kerr, wrote to the company in glowing terms, 'It gives me great pleasure to tell everyone how tremendously admired my twin sets have been here in Hollywood, not to mention how useful they have been to me personally . . . thank you for some lovely cosy days.' Four years later, Edmund Hillary reached the summit of Mount Everest wearing a Hawick sweater to keep him cosy. It was all extremely helpful, sales rose and the town flourished.

Tweed had been woven in the town since the despatch of the allegedly mislabelled package of 'tweel' from Dangerfield's Mill in 1832. And the clever marketing ploy had succeeded. By 1906 there were 14 companies in the town making high quality Scotch tweed. The USA had been a lucrative but fluctuating market sometimes accounting from 70 per cent of output but, with the introduction of import tariffs and stiff competition from elsewhere, sales began to decline. By the mid 1950s, only four manufacturers survived – Wilson & Glenny; Scoon & Hood & Co; Blenkhorn, Richardson & Co; and Robert Noble & Co. Even sharper contraction has reduced tweed making in Hawick to only one manufacturer – Teviotex at Lovat Mill in Commercial Road.

But elsewhere there was success, even renown. What used to be known as the Unofficial Championship began in Scottish rugby as early as 1865 as the early clubs developed a fixture list. Dominated by the FPs of the fee-paying Glasgow and Edinburgh merchant company schools and the universities, neither Hawick nor any of the Border clubs were involved in it. By the 1870s, *The Scotsman* was publishing results and, at the end of each season, the mathematicians on the sports desk would work out which team should be declared champions. The title was only awarded on the basis of games played between those deemed to be of 'first-class status' and the Border teams were definitely seen by the FP clubs as second-class, probably on the basis that they were often beaten by them. But those defeats did not count since the likes of Hawick were not part of the championship fixture list. Daft. Even dafter and more arcane was the rule that the Unofficial Champions were the club who suffered the fewest defeats in matches against other 'first-class' clubs only. This rule remained in place until 1939. The early years of the competition were of course monopolised by the FP teams with either Edinburgh or Glasgow Academicals 'winning' eighteen titles between them from 1865 to 1888.

Eventually Hawick was permitted to compete with the so-called elite and almost immediately became Scottish champions, winning the first of thirteen titles in 1895/96. By 1901, Gala, Jedforest, Melrose, Langholm, Kelso and Selkirk had been admitted. This was no sudden flash of egalitarianism but a reaction to innovation coupled with a visceral fear of the spectre of professionalism. It had already stalked the rugby landscape as the northern clubs in England had broken away and formed the Rugby League. It was a boo-word that none of the scions of the FP clubs wanted to see associated with rugby. But they were to be sore disappointed. Much to the chagrin of the Scottish Rugby Union, the earliest properly competitive rugby union league anywhere in the world was formed in the same year. Hawick, Gala, Jedforest, Langholm and Melrose formed the Border League. Selkirk and Kelso, and briefly Carlisle, joined soon afterwards and until Peebles was admitted in 1996, these seven famous clubs played each other at least twice each season for a century.

As they were for football and cricket in the late Victorian and Edwardian periods, crowds for rugby were huge. The popular bank at Mansfield regularly accommodated thousands of enthusiastic supporters. In fact, enthusiasm boiled over in a Hawick v. Gala match in 1910 when, as usual, the referee was definitely biased in favour of Gala. Supporters flooded on to the pitch and 'a scene of great disorder prevailed, missiles being thrown at the official and the county police had to intervene, as did some of the Hawick players and officials'. The club was forced to endure an entirely unjustified ban from playing within ten miles of Mansfield Park for a month. Quite how that was worked out remains a mystery. All of the grounds of the Border clubs are more than ten miles away, including Gala's Netherdale, that den of iniquity and biased refereeing.

Many away supporters travelled with the Hawick team by rail. Astonishing to recall in the 21st century but, by the late 19th century, all of the Border towns were linked by short railway journeys and, in the 1920/21 season, the secretary of the Border League wrote to the London and North Eastern Railway Company (they had recently taken over the Waverley Line and its branches from the North British Railway Company) asking if special trains could be timetabled to take supporters to matches. And they were.

Hawick Rugby Football Club had enjoyed great success in the first fifty years of its history. Three players had toured to New Zealand and Australia with what was, in effect, the first British Lions team in 1888. They were R. Burnett, W. Burnett and A. J. Laing. In 1900, T. M. Scott had captained Scotland and several other Hawick players had been capped. But it was not until the 1920s that the first truly great team emerged. D. S. Davies, W. B. Welsh and J. Beattie were all regulars in the Hawick and Scotland team. W. R. Sutherland, Wattie Suddie, would undoubtedly have joined them but he did not survive the carnage of Hawick men in the First World War. The club won eight Border League titles and their most glittering period came in the 1926/27 season when Hawick added the Unofficial Championship title to the Border League trophy and they won a grand slam of all the spring sevens tournaments. But, by the early 1930s, many of the great names had retired, the team began to break up and the years before the Second World War saw a relatively fallow time.

Support of another sort existed in Hawick beyond the enthusiastic crowds at Mansfield Park. The manufacture of manly support by Lyle & Scott had an unlikely beginning. It depended initially on the ingenuity of an 'apparel engineer' and the sluggishness of shop assistants on a cold day. On 19 January 1935, as the worst blizzard of the winter whipped off Lake Michigan and whistled through the snowy streets of Chicago, the city's largest department store made a stuttering start to what would become a retail revolution. In one of the huge windows of Marshall Field's, a curious innovation was on display. Instead of cosy, comfy long johns, the store proposed to sell briefs for men, an invention called 'jockey shorts'. The senior management took one look at the window display and another out of the window at the freezing winter weather. This was a crazy idea. Whose idea was it to sell such skimpy items? And they ordered that these ridiculous jockey shorts be removed immediately. From the window.

But immediately took an hour or so and, in that time, Marshall Field's sold 600 pairs of these newfangled cotton briefs. By the end of March, 30,000 pairs had flown off the shelves and a revolution was born. Its ripples were to reach Hawick very soon afterwards.

Known in the USA as jockey shorts, the name derived not from the obvious need for jockeys to keep their vital parts clear of a bouncing saddle but from the word 'jockstrap'. These pouches attached to a thick elastic waistband with only two tapes on either side of the backside to keep it in place were used by sportsmen but they inspired Arthur Kneibler, an apparel engineer for Cooper Inc. of Chicago. He believed, for whatever reason, that men needed support, sporting or not. And, in addition, the Y-shaped fly front on the new jockey shorts made a visit to the lavatory less of a fiddly business. So long a staple of the Hawick hosiery industry, long johns were on their way into history – the sort of item later worn by old geezers such as Corporal Jones or Albert Steptoe.

With commendable speed and business acumen, Lyle & Scott seized the opportunity and negotiated with Cooper & Co to buy a licence to manufacture jockey shorts in Britain – except they were quickly labelled as Y-fronts. And they were an immediate success. When Lyle & Scott's beautifully made products went on sale at Simpson's of Piccadilly, 3,000 pairs a week were sold. Production accelerated and one of the first to be involved on the factory floor was Miss Ellen Irvine of Allars Crescent. She would later remark that she had spent much of her life in manly support of one sort or another.

The success of Y-fronts was unusual – a welcome relief from unrelenting gloom. The 1930s saw a worldwide depression with even the mighty American economy enfeebled by the Wall Street Crash and its long aftermath. In 1932, unemployment in Hawick stood at approximately 1,600 – five times what it had been five years before. But, once again, war stimulated demand and, in the late 1930s, the mills stirred into production. The Second World War was to hurt Hawick much less grievously than the First. Not only did Winston Churchill and his war cabinet understand that a citizen army would never again submit to the wholesale slaughter of the trenches, the conflict was also much more dynamic as the German strategy of blitzkrieg swept resistance aside from 1939 to 1941.

One of the very first actions of the war involved two Borderers – fighting on opposing sides. In October 1939, the Luftwaffe launched their first raid as a squadron of Junkers bombers targeted the docks at Rosyth on the northern shore of the Firth of Forth. Spitfires from 602 and 603 squadrons were scrambled to intercept them and one of the first pilots in the air was Albert Barton from Newstead, near Melrose. It was a daylight raid and people in the streets and on the quaysides of Leith, Granton and the Fife ports watched the dogfights over the firth. The RAF fighters shot down two of the Junkers bombers and badly damaged several others. One managed to limp across the North Sea to Holland but it crashed on landing, killing the aircrew. On board was Frederick Hanson. Known as Sunny, he had been born and raised in Newstead by a Scottish mother and a German father. After the First World War, Hermann Hanson, a hairdresser in Melrose, was forced to return home because of strong anti-German sentiment, some of it forcefully expressed. In a cruel twist, Albert Barton and Sunny Hanson almost certainly knew each other.

As the most terrible of all wars ebbed and flowed across continents, Hawick men fought alongside their comrades in several regiments but many had enlisted in the King's Own Scottish Borderers. Mercifully, they fared no better but no worse in the great conflict and far more men returned in 1945. In some ways, the Second World War had a much greater impact on the home front than the First. While the drama of events overseas affected the people of Hawick deeply, their lives and their town were changing radically. In 2004, some interviews were recorded for a TV series entitled *Borders at War*. Inevitably, only a small fraction of what was said by Hawick people appeared on screen but what follows offers a much more full account of this fascinating period of history by those who saw it happen.

Madge Elliot was eleven years old when war broke out:

I can remember the day that the war was declared by the Prime Minister, Mr Chamberlain, and my mother was very upset at the time. And it wasn't long after that that the siren went in Hawick, and my brother was a scout and he had to don his scout uniform, get his bike out and off he went on his bike. My mother was crying as she thought she would never see him again. So that was the first day you knew of the war. But I was young and everything seemed just to swing into action.

Isa George also had vivid memories:

I was 16 years of age and it was on 3rd September 1939. And I had an older sister called Mary who was pregnant and I was asked to look after her because her husband had been called up a fortnight beforehand. He was in the Reserves. And that's when the first siren went – on 3rd September. What a noise it made. Anyway Mary had been at a neighbour's house and she came back crying because the war had started. You see she had been in the 1914 war as well – she kent what was coming.

When war was declared, the government feared an immediate bombing campaign against Britain's cities. That was a principle of blitzkrieg – an intensive bombardment before a ground attack. And many children were evacuated from the major cities. Madge Elliot again:

I remember also they brought evacuees from the Edinburgh area and my mother took us to Commercial Road and they marched them from the railway station along to one of the school halls to try and get them fixed up with people to stay with. There was quite a number, but I think a lot of them went back home after a wee while.

Isa George recalled Stobs Camp:

> Then all the soldiers came to Stobs, and the military had been there before the war. And we all went to the dances. They were good and that's how I learned to dance – and my dance was ballroom dancing, the Tango, Quickstep, Foxtrot, Old Time Waltz. And we used to have ankle competitions as well. That was in the Drill Hall. You had to stand behind this sheet thing and I won about ten bob because of my legs and my ankles. During the war I didn't bother much about stockings because they were all [available only] on coupons and if you were at a dance and got a kick it was finished. So I used to go to Hamilton the chemist and buy tan in a bottle, and my man used to rub it on and he used to take the pencil and put on the seam.

Madge Elliot again:

> I'll tell you this, the Hawick lassies had a ball! There were thousands of troops at Stobs Camp and more at the Wilton Camp, where the police headquarters are now and at Silverbuthall. And of course church halls were taken over as well. There were dances at the ballroom in the Tower Hotel and in the ballroom at the Crown Hotel, and they used the Town Hall, the Drill Hall and other wee halls. There were dances three or four times a week.
>
> And then of course we had three picture houses then as well, and they were open on a Sunday night, really because of the soldiers for entertainment for them. But then we had a railway and they used the train to get up from Hawick Station to Stobs. And those that missed it, you know, taking a girl home and they missed it. They used to have to walk up over the hills to the camp.

At the beginning of the war, Isa George had to grow up fast:

Now my father died when he was 54. He was in the 1914 war and he suffered a lot. That was in July 1940. After my Dad was buried, I was the breadwinner.

Now, when I started to work my wage was 9 shillings and 5 pence. We used to work 48 hours a week for that but when the war came, we worked longer because we were making these heavy jumpers, khaki, navy and air force blue in the mill. Now I took another job at the little theatre [a cinema] in Hawick. And I ran from the mill down to Croft Road and went in to see the manager, Mr Hill, and then I went up the stair and took the tickets for the balcony. Now I did that for a while because my younger sister was still at school. It was just to help my mother out, poor soul, she only got ten shillings for a widow's pension.

Towards the end of the war, Madge Elliot began work:

The mills were busy enough because they were getting orders from the forces. I started work in the counting house of Robert Pringle and Son Limited. And I remember that up in the underwear department they had big orders for the army. Everybody seemed to be working. It was then that women really started to go out to work. Their husbands were away at the war and there were a lot of women who hadn't been out working before and they had jobs for themselves. I started in 1942 and there were a lot of women working on frames in Pringle's and even some of the knitting machines. They weren't powered machines but hand knitting machines. And women working in Hawick? It's never stopped since.

Isa George met her husband at a dance at the Town Hall:

My friend said, 'Oh, look at those smashing-looking fellas, they're all awful smart.' She said, 'Look, here's one of them coming for us!' Well, when he came across, who did he stop beside? Could I have this dance? Oh yes. So I got up and I said, 'I thought you could dance.' He said, 'I'm just learning.' So we did 1, 2, 3 turn, 1, 2, 3 turn, ye ken. I said, 'I'm fair exhausted.' Now I kent him a while and he kept asking me from the first to marry him. Finally, I said, 'I think we will.' I was only 19 and we got married on 21st March 1942, and he only got 48 hours, that's all he was allowed.

However, when I got word about him being killed, it was a neighbour that came up to tell me because my mother was getting on. I cannae mind of walking from the mill down to our house. I got such a shock because I couldn't believe it.

These everyday tragedies haunted Hawick and the response of many was to work hard to ensure victory. Metal was in short supply and Madge Elliot recalls the effect:

Housewives were asked to donate their aluminium pans and of course they took the railings down everywhere. If you go around, you can see where they've been outside the schools, outside churches, and a lot of nice ornamental railings and they've all just disappeared. That was the war effort.

Actually Britain had nothing at the beginning of the war. In fact if Hitler had done the right thing by his German people, he would have crossed the Channel after Dunkirk and he would have walked through this country. Britain had nothing.

But I just always knew we would win. You were young and daft to think that, I suppose. But it was hard going.

My husband, whom I didn't know then, of course, but he was called up the day France fell, and he was in the RAF and they didn't have a gun to give him. He was given a pike. That's how desperate Britain was.

News was easier to come by in Hawick than it had been during the

First World War because some people had wirelesses and they shared news – especially if it directly affected them. Madge Elliot again:

> Well, we had a wireless. A lot of people didn't have wirelesses in those days but my mother was always keen on these things. I had a second cousin who was on the minesweeper, *Gracie Fields*, and it went down at Dunkirk. He lived with my great aunt who was his granny, and that was how she learned he'd died. It was on the news on the wireless that night. So my mother put her coat on and ran away to see her aunt.
>
> When Winston Churchill became Prime Minister, his speeches just lifted the nation . . . wonderful to listen to him. Even as a girl, you know, 'Fight on the beaches' and so on. I could imagine them all. Even though they were fighting on the beaches, I was always sure that they would win.

As the war wore on, rationing became tighter but Isa George remembers how it could be eased:

> My mother was a country woman and she had a brother and they were in the country and so we never had to look for different things – butter and things like that. And my mother always shared them out amongst the neighbours. That was the only way you could survive. And you only got so much sugar in the week. And eggs were a problem, but it was a funny thing, and I'm still the same. I used to say to my mother, 'Tell you what, you give me the white and you can have the yolk.' I never liked the yolk of an egg. We used to split it between us.

Neighbourliness was indeed a means of survival in the close-knit community of Hawick. Madge Elliot:

> We never went hungry of course because my dad was a poacher.

> We were brought up on salmon and rabbits, poached salmon and rabbits . . . and I'm not talking about the cooking either! And we shared things. I had friends and there were ten of them living in two rooms and you know they had a hard time in the 1930s.
>
> But my friend went away to Australia after the war and she came back and she said to me, 'I'll never forget your dad, Madge. He fed the whole street, a half salmon for this one and a rabbit for that one.' And that was the way we helped each other in those days.

After the loss of many lives, the anxiety of those left at home, the long years of rationing and the privation, the allies at last invaded France in June 1944. Madge Elliot recalls experiencing it twice:

> I remember D-Day and it was on the news on the radio and it was in the papers. But I'll tell you it didn't affect me as much at the time as it did last year when I was watching it on television. I saw more than I was aware of when it happened. And last year it brought a tear to my eye – what these troops and young lads went through. Awful. And some of them in their late teens. Terrible.
>
> I remember being at the Little Theatre, the Wee Thee we called it in Hawick, and the newsreel came on, the Pathé News came on, and they showed our troops entering Belsen. You could have heard a pin drop in that cinema. It was awful. We couldn't believe what we were seeing. And that was Belsen. Couldn't believe it that human beings would do that to other human beings.

The end of the war came in 1945 but the relief from all that suffering was tempered by difficult homecomings. After the frantic period of production to supply the armed forces, the Hawick mills saw a dramatic fall in business. Madge Elliot recalls bitterness and disappointment as soldiers who had risked their lives returned to discover that there was no work:

> It was difficult for employers to accept them all back . . . but some of them were not treated well. My own brother and my husband weren't treated well. So it wasn't a case of opening their arms and saying, 'Welcome home and welcome back to the firm.' It wasn't like that. My husband was a designer, a tweed designer, and again there were too many tweed designers so he wasn't welcomed back. But after a couple of years studying he went away to university and left the tweed design and became a maths teacher.

Nationally, there was a determination not only that there would not be a post-war slump, as had happened after the First World War, but also that society would need to change radically. To the astonishment of the world and of the great war leader himself, Winston Churchill was decisively rejected by the electorate. The returning soldiers, many voting by post, wanted change. Their rationale was clear. Within a generation, there had been two world wars, enormous suffering and economic stagnation, and there was a widespread sense that those who had run the country in the past had failed. The future had to be different and it had to belong to the people. Labour won a famous landslide victory in 1945.

During the war, the Beveridge Report had advocated a National Health Service free at the point of need and, by 1950, it had been achieved. The resistance of doctors had been overcome 'by stuffing their mouths with gold', according to the Minister for Health, Aneurin Bevan. Consultations, prescriptions, dentistry, spectacles and much more – all of these had cost money before the war, money that few could afford, and now they were free. Nationalisation of the coal industry and much of the transport sector took place, and the lives of ordinary people in Hawick were much improved by the policies of, arguably, the most radical government ever elected in Britain.

The National Health Service saved the life of Hawick's most famous son. Having served with the Royal Artillery in the war, he returned to playing rugby for Hawick and, in 1947, played in a Scotland trial.

To experienced observers, it looked as though Bill McLaren would be selected for Scotland but illness intervened. He contracted tuberculosis, a potentially fatal condition. At the sanatorium at East Fortune in East Lothian, he was prescribed streptomycin, an experimental drug, and it saved his life. With a return to rugby out of the question, perhaps the next best thing for McLaren was commentary, and he began with hospital radio at East Fortune and table tennis matches.

Once he had qualified as a physical education teacher and returned to Hawick, McLaren began a distinguished career first as a journalist, gaining early experience at the *Hawick Express* and then as a broadcaster. Commentating first on radio, from 1953, and then on television, from 1959, he was immediately impressive, with a deep rugby knowledge obvious to all who listened. Almost obsessive in his preparation for international matches, compiling large sheets of stiff paper with every fact, statistic and comment that could possibly be relevant, McLaren brought a new dimension of professionalism. And, at the time he began broadcasting, he had serious competition. The early years of television sport produced several talented commentators who became very closely identified with their sport, so closely that it need not be added to their names – Peter O'Sullevan, Dan Maskell, Peter Alliss and Harry Carpenter.

As with Alliss and Maskell, the fact that McLaren had played his sport to a high standard informed his commentary greatly but what made him unique was his remarkable even-handedness, balance and fairness. His career bridged the amateur and professional eras but it was his instinctive love of the game that echoed in his voice. And that was a love born in Hawick. As was his voice, surely one of the richest, most textured and most mellifluous ever heard on television. When Bill McLaren died in 2010, it was the end of several eras.

Beyond the town boundaries, the landscape around Hawick saw radical changes after the end of the Second World War. In 1920, the Forestry Commission was created to restore woodland that had been cut down to meet the needs of war and planting had been started at Kershope near Newcastleton and elsewhere. Because of its hardy nature as a native of Alaska, Sitka spruce was preferred. But it did not flourish until ribbon ploughing was developed. This technique created deeper furrows for better drainage and it also happed up the warming soil around the roots of the saplings. However, there was an unintended consequence of the deep ploughing – one still felt today. Better and faster drainage off the hillsides caused flash flooding and this could be particularly acute in the lower Teviot. 1952 saw severe floods in Hawick with water running along Buccleuch Street.

By the end of the Second World War, about 5 per cent of the land area of the Borders was afforested but, by 2000, this had risen to a staggering 14.5 per cent. Much of the planting is aged Sitka spruce, hardy but ugly. New guidelines have insisted on greater variety but the heritage of two world wars will take time to dissipate. Around Hawick, the effect can be particularly baleful in the Wauchope and Craik Forests, the dense regiments of evergreens standing in rectilinear blocks with arrow-straight rides between them. They have created a sterile environment and their severe geometry imparts an unnatural look to the landscape. Admittedly attitudes and practices are changing but it will take generations for the pine forests to soften.

Harry Ferguson was a genius and, like James Small before him, he changed farming for the better. An Ulster Scot, Ferguson developed a small, affordable tractor that was tremendously versatile. It carried a three-point linkage that enabled the tractor to power whatever implement it was pulling. Wee Grey Fergies were also cheap and more than half a million were turned out by the Standard Motor Company of Coventry. Their widespread use had clear effects in the Borders. Horse working finally and sadly came to an end and people began once more to move off the land to seek work in towns. These were not only farm workers but also the associated trades. In Border villages, the smiddies closed one by one and much was lost.

Those who came to Hawick usually gained employment. The 1950s were good years in the textile trade. After Otto Weisz's innovations at Pringle and Deborah Kerr and Edmund Hillary's endorsements, knitwear was booming. In 1955, Lyle & Scott hired none other than Christian Dior to design a range of products. In the decades immediately after the war when much emphasis was placed on exports, Hawick was reckoned to be the highest dollar earner per capita in Britain. By 1953, between 80 and 90 per cent of the luxury knitwear made in the town was exported to North America. A decade later, labour shortages forced the mills to open branch factories in towns such as Kelso, Earlston, Duns and Eyemouth. There was also expansion overseas and, as late as the 1980s, Turnbull's of Hawick had a shop in the fashionable Via Tornabuoni in Florence. And, most likely as a result of the coveted mill sales (admission by ticket only) in the 1960s, Hawick was voted one of the best-dressed towns in Britain.

After 1945, heroes needed homes and, when consumer demand and the output of the mills increased, everybody needed homes, especially in Hawick. Prefabs were the fastest answer and, in 1944, an act of parliament promised 500,000. In the event only 157,000 were erected but Hawick benefitted greatly. At Silverbuthall, an estate of prefabs was built on the hillside with views over the town and the Teviot and, for many who had experienced the overcrowding of tenement life or a damp farm cottage, they represented a tremendous improvement in living standards. More than 200 were brought in and quickly assembled at Silverbuthall and each contained what will have seemed like luxuries. There were coal fires with back boilers and these ensured a central heating system and constant hot water. There was a man-sized bath, a built-in oven and, something many prefab dwellers would not see again for years, a fridge, one that ran on gas. Several companies that had been engaged on aircraft and other construction switched to prefabs once the war had ended and soon their walls, roofs and fittings were loaded on the backs of lorries for erection all over Britain. The Labour government of 1945–51 also built more than a million conventional houses and laid the foundations of many housing schemes for the 1950s.

The 1899 Ordnance Survey shows open farmland north of Hawick. It lies on the north side of a road above Wilton Cemetery that still runs over to the Boonraw Burn passing the point where it falls into the Teviot opposite Haughhead. In 1950, these south-facing fields began to change forever as the Burnfoot housing estate was laid out and constructed. Council houses had been built before in Hawick, especially at Linwood on the Slitrig, but the scale of what was planned at Burnfoot was of a different order of magnitude. Building continued into the 1970s and, in 2012, the population was 2,732, a small town.

The early inhabitants of Burnfoot enjoyed the high summer of council housing and maintenance. In addition to internal facilities even better than those of the prefabs, many houses had gardens front and back. Because the estate was a mile from the town centre, a parade of shops opened at Kenilworth Avenue, a church was built in 1955, the Burnfoot Roadhouse opened for business and an excellent primary school still serves the area. With a lovely elevated aspect, Burnfoot was a much sought-after address in Hawick in the 1950s and 60s.

Now, sadly, the picture is different. Especially around the shops and Kenilworth Avenue, Burnfoot has more recently witnessed persistent bouts of anti-social behaviour and petty crime. Second only in the Borders to Langlee in Gala, parts of the estate are very deprived. Central Burnfoot, Ruberslaw Road and the Meadows are now seen as undesirable addresses. Despite substantial efforts at improvement, both by residents and the local authority, many inhabitants fall below the poverty line. Of the population of 2,732 in 2012, approximately 23 per cent lie below that measure and Burnfoot is now found in the lowest quartile of deprived areas in Scotland.

More cheerfully, and positively, Hawick was home to one of the greatest painters ever to work in Scotland. Anne Redpath was determined to make her way as an artist. Perhaps her thrawn sense of purpose was a welcome legacy of living in the town. Her father, Thomas Redpath, was a designer with Robert Noble & Co and, in an era when this was unusual, he encouraged his daughter to attend

Edinburgh College of Art in 1913. But, mindful of the fragility of life as an artist, he wanted Redpath to train as an art teacher. She did not but was undoubtedly influenced by her father in other ways, even inspired by Thomas Redpath's work – 'I do with a spot of red or yellow in a harmony of grey what my father did in his tweed.' But she needed to travel and, between the wars, France was a magnet for young painters. Redpath spent fourteen years in both the north and the south, in the clear light of Provence. When she returned to Hawick in 1934, her subjects included the landscape around the town and her *Frosty Morning, Trow Mill* is wonderfully atmospheric. Still lifes, particularly taking everyday objects as their subjects, also attracted Redpath and her work soon found its way into major collections such as the Tate and the National Gallery of Scotland. Timeless, vivid and often brimming with warmth, her sense of colour had some of its roots in Hawick. Much mourned, Anne Redpath died in 1967.

The 1960s saw political change in the Borders. Apart from a brief interlude in 1950–51 when Archie MacDonald was elected as a Liberal MP, the region had been represented by Conservative MPs. Commander C. E. M. Donaldson sat for the old constituency of Roxburgh, Selkirk and Peebles. And mostly, he did sit. A Donaldson speech in the House of Commons was very rare. Described as 'a mild, unimpressive man', he lived in London and made little effort to find a house in his northern constituency. When Labour regained power in 1964, Donaldson hung on with a much-reduced majority of 1,739. It had been badly dented by a young Liberal candidate who had been persuaded to give up Edinburgh Pentlands to fight what was seen as a more winnable seat. After his first campaign, David Steel did not have to wait long for his second. At the age of only 63, Commander Donaldson died in 1965. At the by-election of March that year, Steel swept to victory, becoming Britain's youngest MP and winning by a thumping majority of 4,607. His task was made much easier by the visits of a number of Conservative grandees. When Sir Gerald Nabarro was asked about the problems of depopulation in the Borders, he confessed he was not surprised – Lord Napier and Ettrick used to employ fourteen domestic servants but now the poor chap was down to only one.

The euphoria of David Steel's victory and what seemed like the passing of another age were tempered by blunt political realities. As a member of a tiny party unlikely to be in government, so it seemed then, he was unable to exert pressure on government to direct public spending to the region. Overseen by the Secretary of State for Scotland, Willie Ross, the Labour administration set up funding for many new infrastructure and development projects in the Highlands and the Central Belt. Gleaming new towns sprang up at Cumbernauld, Irvine and Glenrothes and the Highlands and Islands Development Board was established in 1965. Emblematic of the failure of the Borders to benefit from increased government spending in Scotland was Peel Hospital. Looking more like an army camp, it was a group of wooden huts connected by covered outdoor walkways, some of them without walls. One Kelso rugby player nursing a broken cheekbone was admitted to casualty on a rainy afternoon in 1970 and lying on a trolley, he arrived in a ward more than a little damp. There were no gynaecological or maternity departments and despite excellent nurses and doctors, Peel Hospital simply did not have the facilities to offer services that measured up to their skills. The Borders had to wait until 1988 for a modern hospital to open near Melrose, complete with walls.

In 1969 the last train clanked out of Hawick Station, bound for Carlisle and oblivion. The Waverley Line had been axed in the long aftermath of the Beeching Report and the Borders was condemned to see a vital artery severed. When the train neared Newcastleton, the driver could make out a large crowd on the track and he saw that they had closed the level crossing gates. Led by their minister, the Rev. Bryden Maben, these people had come from Newcastleton and they refused to let the last train pass. The Hawick police were summoned and, when they attempted to clear the track, there were scuffles and the minister was arrested. David Steel was on board and very sensibly he began to negotiate. If the police would release the Rev. Maben, the crowd agreed to move and let the train through.

The heady decades of success in the knitwear and tweed industries in Hawick reached Mansfield Park. The rugby club, universally known as the Greens, embarked on a remarkable and sustained period of dominance. In the years immediately following the war, they had lost several very talented players to rugby league. Jack 'Darcy' Anderson had the unique distinction of scoring two tries against the All Blacks, his blistering pace taking him clear of the normally rock-solid defence, but he turned professional with Huddersfield before going on to play for Great Britain.

The statistics of Hawick's success are extraordinary, even tedious for players from other clubs. Between 1954/55 and 1984/85, the club won twenty-one Border League titles out of a possible twenty-six, they topped the Unofficial Championship eight times between 1954/55 and 1972/73 and, when the six-division club championship sanctioned by the Scottish Rugby Union began in 1972/73, Hawick went on to win it no fewer than twelve times, their last win in that sequence coming in 1986/87. And the club went on the win it again two seasons in a row, 2000/01 and 2001/02.

Great players were, of course, at the heart of these teams. In the 1950s and early 60s, H. F. McLeod, G. D. Stevenson, A. Robson and D. Grant won 100 caps for Scotland between them and this was in a period when no more than four or five caps could be awarded in a season. McLeod accounted for forty of these and he also toured twice with the British Lions as a granite-hard tighthead prop. An excellent sevens player, he also took conversions of the many tries scored by the slightly more fleet-footed of his teammates. So powerful were his legs that he needed only one step of a run-up before launching the ball over the bar.

Great sides breed collective confidence and players who may have been no better than competent at other clubs shone at Mansfield.

And very significantly, Hawick's supremacy in the Scottish club game shifted the centre of gravity away from the FP teams of the cities at last. A good illustration is the career of C. M. Telfer, one of the neatest, most complete stand-offs to play for Scotland. He lived in Edinburgh and had attended the Royal High School but chose to play for Hawick. He had family connections and is related to H. F. McLeod.

What sustained Hawick's long-lasting and relentless success was a seemingly unending supply of rugby talent moving up through the ranks. But, uniquely, Hawick had no second team until the 1997/98 season. Instead, there existed in the town four so-called junior teams whose players were available to be selected for the Greens. They were Hawick Linden, Harlequins, Trades and YM. Below this structure were two semi-junior teams for young players between sixteen and eighteen years of age, Hawick Wanderers and Hawick PSA (Pleasant Sunday Afternoon – a pleasing reminder of Corinthian attitudes to sport) and there was a senior team from Hawick High School. This formidable arrangement purred like a Rolls Royce engine for decades.

Perhaps the greatest, most skilled of all Hawick's halfbacks and three-quarters of the post-war era was J. M. Renwick. A beautifully balanced and incisive runner, his skills were matchless as he gained fifty-two caps for Scotland. Renwick was a complete player, able to beat a man with a sidestep or sheer pace over ten yards, or kick from hand or take place kicks. And he was a classic low tackler (although, if the occasion demanded, a highish one too). One illustration suffices. At Murrayfield, he made a line break against England, got half through, reaching the twenty-two. Support was slow and Renwick was checked but there was no English cover to his left and so he threw out a long, looping pass to no one. It bobbled for a moment before being gathered by a teammate sprinting to stay with the gifted Renwick and he touched down.

The undoubted talents of H. F. McLeod were often invisible, buried in the murky half-light of the scrummage and, in the relative sterility of international rugby in the 1950s and early 60s, with its endless set pieces on muddy winter afternoons, there was little open play. But a tighthead prop is still the anchor of a team and McLeod was certainly steadfast. Less well remembered was T. O. Grant, a tremendously physical but skilful back row forward. And the great Adam Robson was unforgettable. When it was remarked that he seemed to be everywhere on the pitch, this most modest of men insisted that it was his bald head that made him more noticeable.

Rugby fortunes ebb and flow and, while they have recently regained their rightful place in the first division of the Scottish club championship, Hawick are not the force they once were. Professionalism has played a role in that decline but the world seems strangely out of kilter without a dominant Greens team. And Scotland are undoubtedly the poorer for it. As a Provost of Hawick once remarked, a good Scotland team is like soup – no good without a lot of green in it.

In the early 1970s, storms were gathering in the economic climate. The Conservative government of Edward Heath faced down the National Union of Mineworkers and Britain found itself short of fuel and forced to work a three-day week. Fundamental structural changes began to ripple through the textile industry in Hawick as family- or locally-owned mills were taken over by larger companies not based in the town. This last was to prove a crucial factor. Joseph Dawson Ltd of Bradford, later to become Dawson International, bought Pringle and Braemar while Courtaulds took over Lyle & Scott. In 1972, mill workers voted to strike in protest at these changes. They feared they could lead to job losses – and they were right. For large companies with their headquarters elsewhere, it is easier to close down production and make people redundant if you are unlikely to meet them in the High Street or in the stand at Mansfield Park. And so it came to pass. As competition intensified and much cheaper goods flowed out of the low-wage economies of India, China and elsewhere, mills in Hawick began to close one by one. 'Rationalisation' is the favoured euphemism for an altogether more brutal process. In 2000, Dawson International sold Pringle to Fang Brothers of Hong Kong and 140 people lost their jobs. Full stops are difficult to find in the tangle of history but this sale did signal an end to a long and proud tradition of textile production in Hawick, that Bailie John Hardie inspired all those years ago.

On Friday 27 February 2004, the Hawick Callants Club held its centenary dinner at the Mansfield House Hotel. To accompany the festivities, the club had republished *Hawick in Song and Poetry*, an updating of the 2001 edition. It is a remarkable historical document. Divided into five sections, it lists thiry-four songs specifically about Hawick or set in the town, a further nine about the countryside around such as Borthwick Water or Teviotdale and finally twenty-five poems listed as being about the Borderland but, in fact, most take Hawick as their theme or were written by Hawick men. And there exist many more not included in this excellent publication.

What is immediately striking is the richness of the Callants' booklet – all that creativity over so many years – and the fact that so little has been lost or forgotten. It is witness to a heroic continuity over many centuries. A starting point for most of the songs and poems with a historical theme is the skirmish at Hornshole in 1514 and this naturally chimes with the antiquity of the Common Riding, the subject of joyful celebration on its quincentenary in 2014. But, if this history shows anything, it is that Hawick is very much older and its origins perhaps more mysterious. The celebrations, the songs and the poems are only the sum, the latest flowering of that heroic continuity.

Talented and weel-kent names decorate the pages of the Callants' collection – names such as James Hogg and Will Ogilvie – but a song and a poem, each written by a Hawick man, are illustrative of something deeper. 'Hawick Stands Alone' was written by George Goodfellow in 1996. Here is part of the third verse and the chorus:

> And since these days of glory,
> We've nailed this message home
> When our town needs defending,
> Hawick can stand alone.

Fearless, strong and true;
She's deep within my heart,
She's inside all of you;
And Hawick can stand alone.

Thrawn, stubborn, conservative and irreducibly different, Hawick is indeed unique and, in the Borders, the town does sometimes stand alone. Not only is the accent singular, doggedly surviving, the town's history followed a different path. Spectacularly successful even in the notoriously fluctuating fortunes of the textile trade, Hawick was the home of invention and innovation. The town produced goods that became world famous and sportsmen who succeeded internationally. Its rugby team and its long period of supremacy in Scotland are perhaps symbolic of Hawick's difference. It combined raw local talent and inventiveness with a grim determination to beat all comers, especially when they came to Mansfield Park. And the club built that dominance in a unique way with no second team of reserves but instead for junior teams of reserves and the sense of pulling on a green jersey as the summit of a playing career, not a means to another end. These are all virtues and, as the bitter winds of economic recession whistle down the High Street, Hawick will need once more to dig deep and embrace them.

For Ian Landles, Hawick is also a summit. A poet, composer, playwright, musician and teacher, Ian aspires to only one description – Hawick Man. He makes much fun out of his love of the town but it is immensely powerful and emotional. Using an original poem about tenement life by Claude Currie as a template, Ian wrote a Hawick version, a very Hawick version, entitled 'Doon Oor Close and Up Oor Stair'. Here it is in full:

A saw a barefit lad the day
And maimory sent iz fer away
Ti times and happenins long since past
The sands o time are rinnin fast

As deep within ma mind a sei
A barefit boy that yince was mei
Doon oor close and up oor stair
Twae cheeny dugs on the mantelpiece
'Ma, can a hev a jeely piece?'
The zinc bath where a weshed ma feet
The cobbled pavement doon oor street
Little o worldly wealth oo hed
A money tin ablow the bed
Claes wi ma brithers a'd to share
Doon oor close and up oor stair
Sunday Schule picnics then
Horse and cairt tae Harden Glen
For the King's tippence oo paid
Or jookeet in doon the arcade
Keystone Cops, Pearl White
Episode three on Thursday night
What different worlds oo experienced there
Frae doon oor close and up oor stair
Dookin for aipples at Halloween
Coats for goalposts in oor back green
Wickets chalked upon the wall
Life Boys in the Pairish Hall
Witter-closet on the stairs
Newspapers cut intae squares
Wi other faimilies oo'd tae share
Doon oor close and up oor stair
The built-in bed where fowre bairns slept
The oothoose where the coal was kept
The Loanheid cockerel, noisy bird
That early in the morn was heard
The auld oil lamp aside the press
The flickerin wick smokeet the gless

Oor Seturday penny spent wi care
Then doon oor close and up oor stair
Cockerossie, off oo ran,
Beds, Guesses, Bools and Kick the Can,
Kep-a-Gush and Gainin Grund,
Skatin on the Curlin Pond,
Girds wad keep oo gaun a while,
Sledgin doon the quarter mile,
They were the ploys o yesteryear
Doon oor close and up oor stair
Then upon the Sabbath day
Tae the Pairish Kirk oo made oor way
Reverend Cathels, grim and dour,
Sermons went on owre an hoor.
'O God our help in ages past,
Make the minister stop.' At last
Oo're back oot intae God's fresh air
Then doon oor close and up oor stair
Monday morning, weshin day,
Wringer and mangle then held sway.
Claes oot on the bleach tae dry
Back Brae craws gaun flyin by.
Up abune, the Mote looks doon
Standin guaird owre a the toon
Naebody'd thought whae' built eet there
Doon oor close and up oor stair
Then yon Friday morn in June
Oo watched the horses roond the toon
Then at the Nipknowes ta'en oor place
Tae sei the stirrin Cornet's chase
At the Mair oo keeked at every stall
On this maist special day of all

And spoke tae neebors whae were there
Frae doon oor close and up oor stair
Simmer mornins off oo set
Catchies baggies in a net
Dookin in the Spetch was braw
Divin off the Dunk Wa'
Chitterin, oor shivery bite oo ate
Didni get back hyim till late
Ma wad be roused, oo didni care
As oo went doon oor close and up oor stair
The railway's disappeared for guid
Car park where the King's yince stood
Pairish Kirk is hooses now
Folk irni the same somehow
Now as a reach ma final page
A look back ti a bygone age
Yet still a can hear ma mother's cry
'Come in, eer bedtime's lang since by'
And in ma mind a sei again
A barefit boy in Myreslawgreen
Gaun ditterin hyim, withoot a care
Doon oor close and up oor stair.

Not only is it possible to hear Ian's rich Hawick voice, it is also easy to recall the lost world he describes so beautifully. Certainly the poem bathes in the warm waters of nostalgia but that is part of Hawick's legacy. Alongside the thrawn determination, there co-exists something altogether softer – what Ian catches so well in the rhythmic verses of his poem. The body warmth of Hawick culture has certainly changed since kids 'dooked' in the Teviot and played 'gainin grund' round the Mote but it survives in the smiles, the handshakes and kisses at the Common Riding, the generosity, the encouragement of young people (surely a central part of the gift of the Common Riding to the town) and also the wonderful sense of humour characteristic of the town and its people. But much more than these elements, the unconscious impulse of togetherness – 'oor close and oor stair' – the active and powerful idea of the community of Hawick still burns with a fierce and warm light – *oo* still means 'us, all of us'.

Over at last fourteen centuries, from when Saegifa and Rosfritha walked up the Slitrig out of Christian devotion, to the brilliance of Otto Weisz and the drama at Mansfield, the idea of *oo*, of a community, has formed and changed in the town. Because of that dogged togetherness, Hawick has a clear and unambiguous identity and it is its greatest strength. Tradition speaks loudly and sometimes what has aye been can seem to inhibit change. But, if this history shows anything, it shows that Hawick has changed radically over the many centuries since people began to live between the Slitrig and the Teviot. All that experience in one place has created and invented much and the future will turn for the better for a simple reason. Hawick's greatest invention is her people.

INDEX

Ad Murum, Bede's birthplace 'at the Wall' 56
Adam, Bishop of Caithness and Abbot of Melrose 74
Adam, the Chamberlain 70
Adderstonesheils 54
Addinston 40, 49
Aethelfrith, King of the Bernicians 39
Aethelwald Moll 60
Agricola 30, 31, 32
Agricultural Revolution 122
agrimensores (land surveyors) 34
Aidan 43, 53
Aimar, the Gallovidian 70
Aitken Turnbull Architects 145
Alba, kings of 62
Alexander I, King of Scotland 67
Alexander III, King of Scotland 73, 75
Alison, J.P. 143, 144, 145
All Blacks Rugby 176
Allan Water 22, 26
Allars Crescent 129, 134, 138, 150
Alliss, Peter 170
Alnwick 85
Alwyn, the Chaplain 70
American Civil War 138
Ancrum 31, 100
  kirkyard at 61, 62
Anderson, Jack 'Darcy' 176
Angeln of southern Denmark 39
Angles 39, 51
  Saxons and 55
Anglian Hawick 51, 56
Anglian ox-gangs 51
Anglians of Deira 39
Anglo-Saxon Chronicle 61
Anna, Duchess of Buccleuch and Monmouth 98, 113, 114, 119
Annan River 28
Annandale 31, 32, 33, 36, 71
Antonine Wall 35, 36, 49, 56
Archaeological Society 142, 145
Argyle pattern 157
Argyll, Earl of 3
Arimathaea, Joseph of 42
Armstrong, Johnnie of Gilnockie 101, 102

Armstrong, Kinmont Willie 104, 105
Armstrong, Willie 114
Armstrong family 100, 103, 106
Ascelin, Lord of Breherval in Brittany 65, 67
Asia Minor 30
Athelstan 62
Atlantis 18
Auchinleck 111
Auld Brig 110
Auld Mid Raw 51, 52, 100, 109, 124, 148
aurochs 14, 15, 16
Avalonia 9, 10

Back Raw 51, 109
Balaclava, Battle of 156
balaclava headwear 156
Baliol, Edward 77
Baliol, Sir Henry 76
balsam plants 147
Baltica 9, 10
Bamburgh 39, 41
  rock of 39
Bannockburn, Battle of 75, 76, 77, 78
Barbour, John 76
Barclay, Miss Margot 152
Bareless Rig 2
Barmoor 85
Barmoor, English camp at 4, 85
barnekin (courtyard) 96, 97
Barony of Hawick 7, 70, 71, 72, 81–2, 119
Barrow, G.W.S. 47
Barton, Albert from Newstead, Melrose 162
bastle houses 95–6, 98
Bateson family 100
Beattie, J. 160
Beattie, William 152
Beck, William 125, 126, 130
Bede of Jarrow 39, 53, 54, 56
Bedlingtonshire 47
Bedrule, east of Hawick 30, 61, 62
Beeching Report 175
Belford 122, 125
Bell family 100
Belsen 168
Bemersyde 43
Ben Lomond 11
Beowulf 57, 58
  Anglian halls described in 57
Berewich or 'Barley Farm' 19
Bernaccia or *Bryneich* (Old Welsh names for 'Land between the Hills') 41
Bernicia 41, 60
  kings of 43
  overlords of 46
  shires of 46–7
  warbands from 42
Bernicians 39, 40, 41, 42
Berrybush 50
Berwick-upon-Tweed 19, 33, 76, 81
  Chamberlain at (tax collector) 80
  place name of (Berwick derived from 'Barley Farm') 45–6
  quays at 71
Berwickshire 12, 32, 55, 85
Bethoc 30
Bevan, Aneurin 169
Beveridge Report 169
Bewcastle 36, 72, 99

Birrens 36
Bishop Adam 74
Bishops of Durham 50
Black Death 80
Black Tower of Drumlanrig 97, 98, 99, 104, 110, 113
Blenkhorn, Richardson & Co. 158
Board of Trustees for Manufacture 123
Bonchester Bridge 4
Bonsor, James 137
boon-work 46–7, 67
Boonraw 50
Boonraw Burn 47, 173
Border Commission 106, 107
Border History (Ridpath, G.) 102
Border League Rugby 141, 159, 176
border reivers 4, 49, 84, 87, 90, 95–6, 99–101, 102–3, 104–5, 106, 107, 113, 114
borderers 10, 15, 16
  on both sides in first World War II action 162
  deaths at Flodden of 4, 87
  flight from Flodden of 3
  at Flodden 86–7
  professional rugby players from among 142
  reiving, effect on 94
  rugby internationsists from among 141
Borderland, poems about 179
Borders
  abbeys 74
  abbots of Border Abbeys 71
  afforestation 171
  agricultural change 121
  Anglian colonisation 49–51, 57
  archaeology 28
  bastle houses 95–6
  Beeching Report 175–6
  Bernician power base 60
  Border Commission 107
  burghs of barony 82
  Christianity, early years of 45, 53–4
  damage to Border abbeys 99
  depopulation 174–5
  Flodden and effect on 84–7
  freak rainstorm in 32
  geography 21–2
  geology and landscape 10–11
  mosstroopers 107
  peel towers 96–7
  place names 19, 27, 30, 38, 45–6
  political change (1960s) 174
  prohibition of use of name by James VI 106
  Roman colonisation 30–36
  Royal expeditions 101, 102–3
  rugby, early beginnings 116–17, 140
  shire organisation 46
  townsmen and countrymen, growth of division between 118–19
  truce day at Kershopefoot (March 17, 1596) 104–5
  unique nature of Hawick in 180
  Wardens of the Marches 89, 93, 103, 104, 105
  warfare 75–80
  wildwood 10
  World War I, effects in 151–3

Borders at War (TV series) 162
Borders General Hospital 175
Borthaugh Hill 33
Borthwick (derivation from 'Byre Farm') 46
Borthwick Mains 46
Borthwick Water 29, 32, 33, 46, 50, 179
Borthwickshiels 46
Bothwell, Earl of 114
Bourne, Geordie 91
Bourtree Place 111, 132, 143, 144
bourtrees or elders 111
Bowden 112
Bowhill House 116, 117
Bowling Club Pavilion 144
Bowmont Valley 89, 122
branch factories 172
Branxholme 71, 76, 81, 100
Branxton 86
Branxton Hill 1, 2, 4
Breteuil, William de 65
Bretwaldas 55, 59
Bridei, King of Picts 60
Bridgehaugh Mill (Selkirk) 151
Brigantes 28, 31, 32, 37
Brigantia 37, 38
Britain 15, 19, 20, 25, 28, 36, 44, 113, 139
Britannia 30, 36, 55
British Empire 131, 133
British Lions 176
Brodie, George of Greatlaws 118
Bronze Age 44
Brougham Place 111, 144
Bruce family 67
Brudenell, James 156
Bruis, Robert 71
The Brus (John Barbour epic) 76
bubonic plague 80
Buccleuch, Dukes of 116, 117, 119, 129
Buccleuch, Scott family of 101, 103, 116, 117, 119, 129
Buccleuch Mill 134
Buccleuch Park 136
Buccleuch Street 130
burgesses 1, 82, 84, 119, 129, 131
Burgh Hill 22, 23, 24, 25, 26, 28, 42
  hillfort on 27
Burgh Muir of Edinburgh 84
Burn, Geordie 89, 90, 92, 95
Burn, Jock 89, 90, 93
Burnett, R. 160
Burnett, W. 160
Burneville, Robert de 70
Burnfoot housing estate 173
Burnfoot Roadhouse 173
Burnford 83
Burning Bush 42
Burnswark Hill 35
Burton-on-Humber 122

Caddon Water 62
Caddonfoot (near Galashiels) 80
Caesar, Julius 30
Caithness 27
Calchvynydd (Chalk Hill in Old Welsh) 19, 38
'callants' 5, 117
  muster to protect Hawick 6–7
Callants' Ba 115

Callants Club 145, 153, 179
Campbell Clan 157
Canmore, Malcolm II 66
cardigans 147–8, 156
Carey, Sir Robert 89, 90, 92, 93, 106
Carham 63
Car(Ker), Sir Robert 91
Carlenrig 101, 102
Carleton, Sir Thomas 96, 97
Carlisle 31, 37, 52, 56, 78, 131
  Bishop of 95
  Carlisle Bells 113
  Castle of 105, 107
Carnegie, Andrew 143
Carpenter Harry 170
Carter Bar 31, 33
Carterhaugh 117, 118, 140
Cary Castle 68, 72, 73, 77
cashmere 147, 157
Castle Cary, Lord of 66
Cataractonium (Catterick) 39, 41
Cathels, Reverend 182
Catrail 49, 50
Catrawt of Calchvynydd 38, 39
Catterick 39, 41
cattle reiving 4, 49, 84, 87, 90, 95–6, 99–101, 102–3, 104–5, 106, 107, 113, 114
  decisive action by James V against 101
  drowning of reivers 103
Cavers 77, 103
Cavers House 72
Cavers Kirk 72, 73
Cavers Parish 73
Celtic Scotland 28, 66
Central Hotel 143, 144
Cessford Castle, (Ker stronghold between Jedburgh and Kelso) 90, 93
Chaipel Park 54
Chamberlain, Prime Minister Neville 163
Charge of the Light Brigade 155
Charles I 109
Charles II 98
Chauvet 17
Cherbourg Peninsula 67
Cheviot Hill 10
Cheviot River 19
Cheviot watershed 10
Cheviots 28, 31, 32, 36, 38, 41, 50, 71, 89, 93, 95
Chicago 160
Chiswick (derivation of 'Cheese Farm') 46
Christianity
  Christian church 56
  ecclesiae (mother churches of shires) 47
  holy orders *ad succurrundum* ('done in a hurry') 74–5
  inscriptions 45
  spread of 45
Christians 42
Church of Scotland 109, 131
Churchill, Winston 167, 169
Clarkson, Bailie 117
Claudius 30
Clennel Street 89
Clyde River 28, 35
Cobble Cauld 116
coble ferry 109

Cockburn, William of Henderland 101
Coel Hen (Old Cole) 36
Coelius 36
Cogsmill 54, 59
Colbanus 70
Coldstream 14, 33
Cole, Old King 36
Collingwood 94
Colours, Casting at Selkirk of 4
Combination Bill 126
Commercial Road 129
Common 22, 83, 119, 131
Common Haugh 116, 129
common land rights 112
Common Riding 6, 62, 179, 183
  Common Riding Day 84
  horse racing at 113
  Hut at 57
  importance of 112
  quincentenary (2014) 179
  Victorian look, acquisition of 146
common ridings in Border towns 119
Commonwealth War Graves Commission 149
community leadership, post-Flodden lack of 7
Congregational Church 144
Conservative Club 144
constituency (Roxburgh, Selkirk and Peebles) 174
Cooper & Co. 161
Cooperative Society 143
coracles 13
Corbet, Robert 70
Corbett, Jennie of Selkirk 151
Corbridge 31
Cornets 110, 146
Cornet's Chaplain 147
Cornwall 27
Cospatric, brother of Dalphin 70
Cospatric, son of Aldeve 70
Cospatric the Sheriff 70
Cotentin 67
'cotton famine' 139
Count David 68
Courtaulds 178
Covenanters
  faith of 111
  minister's mask 112
Coventry 171
Craigend of Mynto 100
Craik 32
Craik Cross Hill 34
Craik Forest 29, 33, 35, 56, 171
Craik Road 34, 35
Cramond 12, 13, 31
Crescent Quarter 129
cricket, introduction of 136
Crieff 131
Criffel 35
Crimean War 156
Croall, John 99
Croall Bryson & Company 99
Crofts, James 98
Cross Wynd 125
Crown Hotel 164
Crozier family 100
Crumhaugh Hill 68, 138
cult of St Mary at abbeys 74
Cumberland 95
Cumbernauld 175

Cumbria 67
coast of 39
West Cumbria 10
Curle, Alexander O. 68, 69
curraghs 13, 14, 19
Currie, Claude 180
Curthose, Henry 67
Curthose, Robert 67

Dacre, Lord Thomas 3, 5
Dalglish, John 99
Dalkeith Palace 113
Dangerfield Mill 133, 158
Danube River 20
Darnick (derived from 'Hidden Farm') 46
David I 70, 73
Davies, D.S. 160
Davis, Jefferson 139
Dawson International 147, 178
Deans, Cornet George 113
Deans, John 83
Deardon, Edward 147
Deidhaugh 113
Deira 39, 60
Denholm 33
Denmark 18
Derbyshire 126
Dere Street 31, 33, 34, 36, 38, 39, 76, 89
Desert Fathers (Near Eastern monks) 43, 54
Devil's Tree 110
dialect of Scots spoken in Hawick 127, 128
Dickson and Laing's Spinning Mill 130
Dior, Christian 172
Dod Burn 22, 26
Dod Rig 23
Dogger Bank 18
Doggerland 18
dollar earner – Hawick highest in Britain 172
Donald III Ban 66, 67
Donaldson, Commander C.E.M. 174
Doon Hall 57
'Doon Oor Close and Up Oor Stair' (Ian Landles poem on tenement life) 180–83
Dordogne River 15
Douglas, George 150
Douglas, James 150
Douglas, Sir James (The Black Douglas) 76, 77
Douglas, Sir William of Drumlanrig 78, 81–2, 84, 87
Douglas, Tom 150
Douglas family
of Cavers 7
charter 119
Douglas Empire 77
of Hawick 7
Douglas of Drumlanrig, Sir William, Baron of Hawick 3, 7
drainage 121
'drengs' (Bernician officials) 46, 49, 50, 67
Dreux, Yolande de 75
Drinkstone 47, 49, 50
Drinkstone Hill 47
Drumlanrig Square 51, 52, 100, 148

Drumlanrig's Tower 7, 52
Drummond, Margaret 111
Druridge Bay 154
Dryburgh Abbey 43
Dunbar 12
Dune (the Dunion) 48
Dunkirk 166, 167
Dunnichen, near Forfar 60
Dunragit 23
Duns, 'handba' at 115
Durham 49, 72, 80
Durham, Bishop of 67
Durham Cathedral 54, 85
Dux Britanniarum 36
Dye, Robbie 141

Eadberht 60
Eadulf, Earl of Bamburgh 62
Eaglescairnie in East Lothian 47
Earl David 71
Earls of Bamburgh 62
Earls of Northampton and Huntingdon 73
Earlston 14, 81
East Barns 12, 13
East Boonraw 47
East Fortune, East Lothian 170
East Port 52, 116, 117, 138
Eastla 110, 115, 116, 130
Eccles, Berwickshire 47
Eccles Cairn (near Yetholm) 47
The Ecclesiastical History of the English People (Bede) 53
Ecgfrith, King of Angles 60
Ecgred, Bishop of Lindisfarne 48
Eden River 105
Edgar, King of Scotland 67, 68
Edinburgh 12
  castle rock 11, 38, 39
  College of Art 174
  George IV's state visit to 132–3
  Tolbooth 101
Edinburgh Castle 75
Edinburgh Pentlands 174
Edward I 75
Edward II 75
Edward III 79, 80
Edwin, King of Teviotdale and Northumbria 55
Egypt 30
Eild Rig 29
Eildon Hill North 31, 32, 38, 60
  rock of 39
Eildon Hills 10, 31, 33, 34
Eildrig Burn 29
Eildrig Hill 29
eileirg (narrow valley/defile) 29
Eilrig Cottage 29
Elbe River 39
Elizabeth I ('Old Queen Bess') 103, 104
  death of 106
Elliot, Jean 4
Elliot, John 110
Elliot, Madge 162, 163, 164, 165, 166, 167, 168
Elliot family 100, 103, 106
Ellis, William Webb 114, 139
Elmet, kingdom of 37
elrigs/eildricks (narrow valleys/defiles) 29
England 9–10
  border between Scotland and 28
  Christian Church in 42

Civil War in 109
Norman conquest of 65–6
raids into Scotland from 100
Roman colonisation of 30–31
Scottish Wars of Independence with 75–81
textile trade in 132, 135
Union of Crowns with Scotland 106
English Channel 4
Ocean (Roman name for) 30
Eric , King of Norway 73
Esk River 14, 36, 99
Esk Valley 37
Eskdalemuir 35
Esplin, Thomas 136
Etal Castle 85
Ettrick, Yarrow and 101
Ettrick Bridge 117
Ettrick Forest 28
Ettrick Pen 50
Ettrick River 19
Ettrick Valley 117
Euphrates River 20
European Grand Prix circuit 154
Everest, Mount 157
Ewes River 14
Ewes Valley 37
Ewesdale 99, 131

Faldo, Nick 157
Falkirk 131
Fang Brothers, Hong Kong 178
Fastern's E'en (Shrove Tuesday) 76, 115
feisty women of Hawick 72
Ferguson, Harry 171
Fertile Crescent 20, 21
feu-ferme (money rent for land) 46
feudal tenure 73
Fiddes, Jim 136
fitzMalcolm, David 67
Flanders 71, 149
flash flooding in lower Teviot 171
Flemish merchants 71
Flodden, Battle of 1–4, 5, 10, 84–7, 99
Flodden Hill 85
Floors Castle 81
Florence 172
'Flowers of the Forest' (Jean Elliot, 1756) 4
Football Association 140
Football Club 141
Ford Castle 85
Fore Raw 52, 109
Forestry Commission 170
Forster, Sir John, Warden of English Middle March 93, 103
Forth, Firth of 13, 33, 75
Forth River 35
Fortingall, Perthshire 45
France 15, 139
Scotland's Auld Alliance with 4
Free Polish Army 153
French Revolution 126
Frosty Morning, Trow Mill 174
Fynnik -Fenwick 82
Fynnik dyke 83

Galashiels 49, 62, 81
('dirty Gala' epithet) 118
Gallipoli 150, 153
Galloway 67, 111

gasworks, opening of (1830) 132
Gateshaw Braes, Morebattle 111–12
Gatwick (derived from 'Goat farm') 46
Gaul 30
Gedwearde (Jedworth) 48
George, Isa 163, 164, 165, 167
George IV 132
Germany 18
giant hogweed 147
Gillemichael 70
Gladstone Street 150
Glasgow 123
  bishopric of 72
Gleneagles, Perthshire 47
Glenrothes 175
Godfrey, Val 136
Gododdin 37, 39
  citadel on castle rock, Edinburgh 40
  kings of 38, 39
Goldelands dyke 83
Golistan, Lord of Edinburgh 39
Goodfellow, George 179–80
Gracie Fields (minesweeper) 167
Graham, Hutcheon 106
Graham family 106
Grand Historical Pageant, Volunteer Park 152
Grand Prix circuit in Europe 154
Grant, Derrick 176
Grant, T.O. 178
The Grate Rode 33
Gray Coat 23
Green Lane 134
Greenknowe Tower near Gordon 97
The Greens (Hawick R.F.C.) 176, 177, 178
greenstone 24
greywacke 16, 97
'Gritty Ware' 97
Grubenhaus ('sunken house') 59
Grundistone Heights 117
guitterbluids 52, 115–16
Gun Knowe 81
Guthrie, Archie 154
Guthrie, Private James 153, 155

Hadrian's Wall 32, 36, 37, 49, 56
Haegathorn 41
haegtesse (woman with prophetic powers) 41
Haegzusa (spirits known as 'Hedge Riders') 42
Haldane, James 124
Hall, Rob 118
'handba' in Border towns and villages 114
Hanson, Frederick 162
Hanson, Hermann 162
Harbottle 89
Harbottle Castle 90
Harcla, Sir Andrew de 78
Harden Bridge 33
Harden Glen 181
Hardie, Bailie John 121, 123, 125, 135, 179
Harehead 99
Harlequins R.F.C. 177
Harold 66
Hassendean 134
Hastings, Battle of 65
Haughhead 173

Hawick 5, 7, 9, 14, 16, 20, 24, 50, 79, 103, 104, 107, 142
becoming part of realm of Scotland 63
derivation of name of town 41–2
feisty women of 72
Hall in Anglian Hawick 57
'handba' in 114
Langholm rugby fixture with 140
legacy 183
rugby as 'religion' of 114–15
village of (existence by end of 7th century) 54
Hawick Advertiser 142
Hawick and Wilton Cricket Club 140
Hawick Express 170
Hawick in Song and Poetry (Callants Club) 179
'Hawick Stands Alone' (George Goodfellow) 179–80
'Hawthorn Farm' (Hawick) 41–2, 46
Hay, William, Earl of Erroll 3
Heaney, Seamus 57
Heath, Edward 178
'Hedge Farm' 41
Henderson, Dandy 136
henges 22–3, 24, 25, 44
Henry, son of the Earl 70
Henry I og England 67, 70
Henry III of England 73
Henry VIII of England 4, 5, 84, 85
Hepburn, George, Bishop of the Isles 1
Hermitage Castle 78
Heron's Hole (Hornshole) 5
Hexham 95, 100, 107
Hexham Gap 28
Hic iacit Caranti Filii Cupitani ('Here lies Carantus, son of Cupitianus') 45
High Rochester fort 89
High School 129, 177
High Street 113, 114, 138, 178, 180
number twenty-one 125
Highlands 175
Hillary, Edmund 157, 172
Hislop, Steve 155
Hitler, Adolf 166
hogback tombstones 61
Hogg, James 5–6, 62, 132, 179
Holy Blood 42
Holy Grail 42
Holy Thorn 42
Holyroodhouse 133
Home, Earl of 116
Home, Lord Alexander 2, 3, 5
Home family 93, 101
Hornshole 5–7, 121, 152, 179
Hornie's Hole (Hornshole) 5
The Horse 144, 152
horse gear 28
hosiery manufacture 124–5, 127–8, 132, 136, 161
'house- rent' 124
Howdenburn 153
Howegate 109
Hrothgar, King of the Shieldings 57
Huddersfield 142, 176
Hugh de Moreville 70
Hughlands and Islands Development Board 175
Hunewic manor, Somerset 72

Hunt, Alfred 136
Hunt, Henry 136
Hunters (Selgovae) 29
Huntly, Earl of 5
Huntly's Highlanders 3

Iapetus Ocean 9, 10
Iapetus Suture 9, 10
Ice Age, refuges from 15
Ida, King at Bamburgh 39
'Ill Week,' raiding eccesses of 106
Industrial Revolution 10
industrial/urban landscape 134, 148
Innes Henderson (later Braemar) 142
Iona 43, 45
Iraq 20
Irish chroniclers 61
Irland, Robert 114
Irvine, Miss Ellen of Allars Crescent 161
Irvine, William 114, 144
Irvine family 100
Irvine (new town) 175
Isabel (daughter of William de Breteuil) 65
Islandshire 47
Islay Herald 85
Isle of Man TT 154
Italian merchants 71
Italian Renaissance 17
Italy 71

James I of Great Britain and Ireland 104
James II of Great Britain and Ireland 98
James II of Scotland 81
James IV of Scotland 1, 2, 3, 4, 84, 85, 86, 99
James V of Scotland 101, 102
James VI of Scotland 102, 104, 106
Jedburgh 47–8, 67, 77
Castle at 81, 115
'handba,' survival at 115
medieval grammar school at 111
Mercat Cross at 97
Jedburgh Abbey 43
Jedforest 89
Jethart Ba 115
Jethart Justice 107
'jockey shorts' 160–61
'jockstrap' 161
John, Bishop of Glasgow 70
Johnstone family 96, 101
Joseph Dawson Ltd of Bradford 178
Joseph of Arimathaea 42

Kelso 19, 38, 50, 81, 89
medieval grammar school at 111
Kelso Abbey 33, 43
Kenilworth Avenue 173
Ker, Sir Robert of Cessford 90, 93, 94
Ker stronghold near Crailing, burning of 103
Kerr, Deborah 157, 172
Kers of Cessford and Ferniehurst 101, 103
Kers of Greenhead 83
Kershope near Newcastleton 170
Kershopefoot in Liddesdale 104
Keyne, James, bailie 83
Kielder Forest 99

The Kingdom of the Scots (Barrow, G.W.S.) 47
King's Own Scottish Borderers 153, 162
Kirk Wynd 109
Kirkin of the Cornet 147
Kneibler, Arthur 161
knitting frames 123
Knox, John 111

Laidlaw's Cauld 130
Laidlaw's Mill 130
Laing, A.J. 160
Laing, John and Son 137
Lake District 35
Lammermuirs ('Lambs' Moors') 41, 71
Lancashire 37
Landles, Ian 180–83
Landles, J.C.G. 146, 147
landscape 9–11, 13, 18–19, 24–5, 26, 27, 29–30, 34, 35, 50, 66, 72–3, 121, 170–71, 174
  industrial/urban landscape 134, 148
'lang bullets' (popular sport) 113–14
The Lang Stand Oot (strike of 1817) 125, 126
Langdale axes 25
Langdale Pikes, Lake District 25
Langholm 50, 52, 113, 140
  races at 105
Langlands Mill 129
Langlee, Galashiels 173
Lascaux 15, 17
Last Supper, Holy Grail and 42
Lauder 110
Lauderdale 40, 41
Laurentia 9, 10
'Laws of the Marches' 93
Lee, General Robert E. 139
Leeds 37
Leeds Rugby League 142
Leicester 126
Lempitlaw near Kelso 61
Lennox, Earl of 3
Liberal Club 144
Liddel Water 45
Liddesdale 20, 77
Liddesdale Keeper 105
Liège 149
Lieutenant's Tower 110
Life of St Cuthbert (Bede) 54
Lightbody, William 140
Lilliesleaf 51
Lincoln, President Abraham 139
Linden R.F.C. 177
Lindisfarne 43, 45, 48, 53
  Church on 61
Lindsey, Walter de 70
Linton 82
Linwood 173
The Lion (cannon) 81
Little family 100
Little Ice Age 78, 79
The Loan 52
Lochwood Tower 96
Locke, John 133
London and North Eastern Railway Company 159
Longnewton 82
Lord Dacre 87
Lord Home 87, 103

Lord Lindsay 103
Lord of Burgh Hill 27
Lothians 28, 31
Lovel, Alicia 73
Lovel, Christina 72, 73
Lovel, Henry 71, 72
Lovel, Hugh 73
Lovel, Lady Matilda 72
Lovel, Ralph 72
Lovel, Richard 72, 80
Lovel, Sir John 77
Lovel, Sir Richard 77
Lovel, Sir Robert 73
Lovel family 65, 66, 67, 68, 69, 70, 73, 75, 76, 98
Lovels of Hawick 71, 77
Lower Tweed 28
Lucius III 71
Luff, George 143
Lyle & Scott 142, 160, 172, 178
Lyne Water 19, 20, 99
Lynwood Mill 137
Lyulf, son of Uchtred 70

Maben, Rev. Bryden 175, 176
MacAlpin, Malcolm II 62, 63
Macchus 70
MacDonald, Archie 174
macGabrain, Aedan, King of Argyll 40
Mackintosh, Charles Rennie 145
McLaren, Bill 129, 169–70
McLeod, Hugh F. 176, 177, 178
MacMalcolm, David 66, 68
maenorau (estates) 46
Maer, Mormaer (mayor) 46
Maid of Norway 73, 75
The Mair 182
Malmesbury, William of 56
Man, Isle of 9
Manor Valley 46
Mansfield House Hotel 179
Mansfield Park 116, 121, 141, 159, 176, 178, 180, 184
Mansfield Road 129
March Wardens 89, 93, 103, 104, 105
Margaret, saintly Saxon Queen of Scotland 66
Marne, Battle of the 149, 153
Marriot, George 146
Mars and Venus, inscription to 56
Marshall Field's 160
Mart Street 134
Mary, Queen of Scots 102, 114, 119
Maskell, Dan 170
Matilda (Maud) 66–7, 70
Maxwell family 93, 101
The Meadows 173
Meldon Burn 19
Melrose 38, 53
  medieval grammar school at 111
Men's Ba 115
Mercia, kingdom of Offa 55
Merse (northern marches of Northumbria) 55
Mesopotamia 20
Michigan, Lake 160
Middle Shires 106, 107
Midlem (originally Middleham) 50, 51
Milfield Plain 85

mill lades off Slitrig 130, 137
Miller, Elizabeth 111
mills 130, 133, 135, 137–8, 139, 142–3, 148, 151, 156–7, 161, 165
booming times for 139
branch factories, opening of 172
carding and spinning mills 129, 130
cotton mills of Lancashire 139
development of 127
post-war difficulties 168–9
'rationalisation' for 178–9
short time working 156
three-day week 178
Minto kirkyard 34
Mithag, John, Provost of Selkirk 83
Moat of Hawick 52, 97
Moffatdale Hills 96
Monmouth, Duke of 98
Montgomerie, Colin 157
Montgomery, George 150
Montgomery, James 150
Montgomery, William 150
Morrison's supermarket 132
Moses, Alfred 140
Mosspaul 99, 131
watershed at 14
Mosstroopers 107
Mote of Hawick
site of earliest building 51–2, 70, 182, 183
Motorcycle Club 154
motte-and-bailey castles 66, 68, 69, 76
Mumby, Mr 122
Murray, J.A.H. of Denholm 128
Murrayfield 121, 141, 177
Muscamp, Reginald de 70
Museum and Gallery 16
Myreslawgreen 138, 183

Nabarro, Sir Gerald 174
Namur 149
Napier and Ettrick, Lord 175
Napoleon Bonaparte 125
National Gallery of Scotland 174
National Health Service 169
National Union of Mineworkers 178
Netherby 36
Neville's Cross, Battle of 80
New Forest 66–7
New Hudson Motorcycles 154
Newcastle 56, 106
Newcastleton 45, 175
Niarbyl 9
Nipknowes 182
Nisbet kirkyard 61, 62
Nith River 35
Nixon, John 124, 125
Nixon family 100
Noble, Robert & Co 173
Norham Castle 85
Norhamshire 47
Norman Conquest (and expansion) 65, 70
Norse lords 61, 62
North British Railway Company 159
North Northumberland Plain 28
North Sea 11–12, 18, 19, 20, 39, 61
North Tyne Valley 131
North Yorkshire 39
Northumberland 12, 32, 95

Northumbria 54
  kings of 56, 60
  power of 63
Norwood 145

Odardo, Sheriff of Bamburgh 70
Odin
  or Woden (Norse war god) 62
  Thor, Tiw and (pagan gods) 56
Offa of Mercia 60
Offa's Dyke 49
Ogilvie, Will H. 94, 179
Old Gaelic (speech of the Irish) 27
Old Melrose 43, 44
Old Roxburgh 76
Old Welsh (dialects of) 27
Oliver, Andrew 132
Ordnance Survey 173
Ormiston 5
Orm's Hole 5
Orm's Tun 5
Osbert the Chaplain 70
O'Sullevan, Peter 170
Oswin of Northumbria 60
Oswulf, son and heir of Eadberht of Northumbria 60
Outer Silver Pit 18
Outerside Rig 33
Owain, King of Strathclyde 62, 63
Oxford English Dictionary 128

Pagano de Braiosa 70
Palmer, Arnold 157
palus ('beyond the Pale') 69
palus (Latin word for 'stake') 96
Pangea 10
Paris 149
Parliaments, Union of 113, 123
Peden, Alexander 111–12
Peden's Pulpit 112
Peebles 19, 38, 45, 50
Peel Fell 50
Peel Hospital 175
peel towers 96, 99
Penchrise Pen ('Hill of Chrise Hill') 23, 27, 38, 42
Peniel Heugh 27
Pennines 28
Pennygant Hill 27
Pennymuir 27
Penrith 37
Persia 30
Peter Scott's (Pesco) 137, 142
Picasso, Pablo 17
Pictish symbol stones 44
pikemen at Flodden 3
Pilmuir Rig 113
Plantagenet claim 76
Player, Gary 157
pneumonic plague 80
Pontius Pilate 57
Porter brothers, Rinkvale Cottages 150
Potato Famine 128
Potts, John 124
Pow Cup 114, 144
prefabs 172–3
Priesthaugh 22
Pringle, Robert and Son 172, 178
Provence 174
Provost Marshal 92
P.S.A. (Pleasant Sunday Afternoon) 177

pybyll (tents or shelter) 38
Pyrenees 15

'Queen of the Borderland' (Hawick) 152

Radulph, the Englishman 70
Raeburnfoot 35
raiding
  English into Scotland 4–5
  'Ill Week,' raiding excesses of 106
Railway Station 134
Ralton Burn 45
Ramsay, Sir Alexander 77, 78
Raphael 17
Ratho, near Edinburgh 59
'rationalisation' of textile industry 178–9
redbrick lum 137
Reddenburn 103
Redesdale bastle house 89
Redpath, Anne 173, 174
Redpath, Thomas 173, 174
Reformation in Scotland 95, 111
Reginald of Durham 54
reivers 4, 49, 84, 87, 90, 95–6, 99–101, 102–3, 104–5, 106, 107, 113, 114
  drowning of 103
Renwick, J.M. 177
Rheged 37, 38
Rhine River 20
Richard II 70–71
'Riding Times' 94
  see also border reivers
Ridpath, Rev. George 102
Risingham 36
road bowls 114
Robbers' Law 30
Robert de Painton 70
Robert de Umfraville 70
Robert Noble & Co. 158
Robert Pringle and Son Limited 156, 157, 165
Robert the Bruce (de Bruis) 33, 70, 75, 77, 78
Robson, Adam 176, 178
Robson, James 122, 123, 125
Rocesburg (lost medieval city of Roxburgh) 33
Roger de Leicester 70
Roll of Honour for Hawick 152
Roman altar 34
Roman basilica 56
Roman Empire 30, 36, 37, 38, 45
  postal system 35
  roads 33, 34, 38, 56, 76, 89
  survival of Roman installations into 12th century 56
Romans 29, 30
Rome 31, 36
  architectural heritage 55
Rosfritha ('horse friend') 54, 57, 59, 67, 73, 184
Ross, Willie, Secretary of State for Scotland 175
Rosyth 162
Rouge Croix Pursuivant 85
Roughheugh Mill 129
Routledge, Simon 82
Routlesche, Black John 99–100
Roxburgh 19
  market at 71
  Rocesburg (lost medieval city of Roxburgh) 33

Roxburgh, Duke of 112
Roxburgh Abbey 19
Roxburgh Castle 38, 76, 78, 81
Roxburghshire 12, 79
Royal High School 177
Royal Museum of Scotland 24, 112
Ruberslaw 11, 29, 30, 31, 32, 35, 111–12
Ruberslaw Road 173
rugby 114–15, 116–17, 118–19, 129, 139–42, 158, 159–60, 176–7, 178, 180
  Unofficial Championship 158, 160, 176
Rugby Football Union (RFU) 140
Rule Water 4
Rulebethocslaw 30
Rutherford 82
Rutherfurd, John 138
Ruthwell 72

Sachsenring Circuit 155
Saegifa 54, 57, 59, 67, 73, 184
Sandbed 20, 53, 110, 116, 130, 138
Saughtree 131
Scandinavia 18
Sclaterford 4
Scoon and Hood & Co; 158
Scot, John 126
Scotland 10, 11, 16, 18, 35, 113
  central belt of 175
  Church of Scotland 109, 131
  improvement in fishing industry 123
  'Scotland's Aldershot' 153
  Society of Antiquaries 145
  woollen/linen production, improvement in 123
Scots 15, 18
Scots ploo 121
The Scotsman 158
Scott, Adam of Tushielaw 101
Scott, David of Stirches (Stirkschawis) 100
Scott, James, first Hawick Cornet 112
Scott, Lady Sybil 152
Scott, Sir Walter 116, 117, 118, 132, 133
Scott, T.M. 160
Scott, Walter of Buccleuch 105
Scott, Walter of Howpasley 99
Scott, William 140
'Scott Country' 133
Scott tower at Eckford, burning of 103
Scottish Football Union 141
Scottish Reformation 95, 111
Scottish Rugby Union (SRU) 159, 176
Scottish Speed Championships 154
Scotts of Buccleuch 101, 103, 116, 117, 119, 129
Scrope, Lord, Warden of English West March 104, 105
Second World War 17, 160, 161, 162
Sedgemoor, Battle of 98
Selby, Mr 92
sele and *circe* (Anglian words for 'church by the hall' 57
Seleskirkja ('Hall-Church') 19
Selgovae 28, 29, 31, 32, 34, 36, 37
Selkirk 14, 19, 50, 57, 62, 112, 117
Selkirk Abbey 70

Selkirk Common Riding 4
Senlac Hill 66
sewage system, installation of (1877) 142
sheep
  North Country Cheviots 122, 125
  traditional black-faced breed 122
short bullets 114
Silverbuthall 164, 172
Sim the Laird 102
Simprim 33
Simpson's of Piccadilly 161
Sinai 43
Sinclair, Sir John 122
Sitka spruce 171
Skelfhill 84
Skiddaw 35
Slitridge Water 130
Slitrig Crescent 132
Slitrig River 12, 19, 20, 25, 37, 44, 51, 52, 68, 82, 109, 110, 127, 138, 184
Slitrig Road 78
Slitterick ('slitter') 19
Smailholm 82, 96
Small, James 121, 123, 127, 171
smiddies 171
Society of Antiquaries of Scotland 145
Solemn League and Covenant 109
Solway coast 37
Solway Firth 31, 99
Solway fords 76
Solway Moss 31
Somerset 72
South Queensferry 75
The Southern Counties Register and Directory 138
Southern Uplands 9, 28
Soutra Hill 31
Spetch 183
Sprouston 57
St Andrews canons 71
St Cuthbert 48, 53, 56, 74
  banner of 85
St Cuthbert Chapel 59
St Helens Rugby League 142
St Mary's 20, 43, 44, 45, 52, 53, 54, 70, 113, 114
St Mary's Kirk 42, 51, 79
  kirkyard of 84, 125
St Ninian 56
St Patrick 56
St Vigeans Church, Arbroath 44
standard-bearers 55, 112
Standard Motor Company 171
Stanwix Bank 105
Steel, David (Lord Steel of Aikwood) 174, 175, 176
Stevenson, George D. 176
Stewart, Alexander, Archbishop of St Andrews 1
Stewart, James, Earl of Moray 102, 103
Stewart dynasty 67, 111
Stirling castle rock 11
Stobs Camp 152, 164
Stonehenge 23
Stranraer 23, 37
Surrey, Thomas Howard, Earl of 2, 85, 86
Sussex, Earl of 103, 104
Sutherland, W.R. 160

Swale River 39
swing plough 121, 127
Symeon of Durham 48, 60, 63
Synton Moss 14
Syria 20, 43

ta (pre-Celtic word) 19
Tain River 19
Tate Gallery 174
Tay, Firth of 31
Tay River 19
Telfer, C.M. 177
Teribus Ye Teri Odin 5–6, 61–2
Teridom, Teris and 54, 62
Terra Lindisfarnensis (estates of church of St Cuthbert) 49
Teviot River 5, 6, 12, 16, 19, 20, 25, 35, 37, 38, 44, 48–9, 51, 52, 68, 82, 116, 129, 138, 184
  flash flooding in lower Teviot 171
Teviot Valley 12, 16, 33, 56, 131
Teviotdale 4, 20, 21, 30, 34, 41, 43, 47, 49, 50, 60, 61, 62, 67, 72, 76, 87, 94, 96, 99, 179
  dialect of 128
  Leisure Centre 134
  Sheriffdom of 78
Teviotex at Lovat Mill 158
Teviothead 14, 16, 155
Teviotmouth (Kelso) 48
Thames River 19
thegns (Bernician officials) 46–7, 50, 55
Therouanne 84
Thomas Brydon and Sons' windows and ingo doorway 145
Thomas of Ercildoune (modern Earlston) 50, 51
Tigris River 20
Till River 86
Tinchebrai 67
Titus, Emperor 31
Tolbooth 110, 111
Torwoodlee 49
Tournai 84
Tower Hill 98
Tower Hotel 99, 138, 164
Tower Knowe 110
Tower Mill 137
Town Council 123, 146–7
Town Hall 134
Townhead Port 52
Trades R.F.C. 177
traditions 52, 58–9, 61–2, 72, 146–7, 153, 184
'traitors of Levyn' 99, 100
Transactions of the Hawick Archaeological Society (1951) 146
transhumance 83
Traprain Law, East Lothian 38, 39
Trimontium 34–5, 38, 56, 60
T-rivers 19
Troutlawford 83
Turnbull's of Hawick 172
Turvill, Harry 136
Turvill, John 136
Tweed basin 18
Tweed Forum 147
Tweed River 14, 19, 20, 32, 38, 43, 71, 86, 89
  Lower Tweed 31, 76
Tweed Valley 12, 16, 33, 39, 40, 55

Tweeddale 4, 21, 41, 43, 50, 60, 67, 94, 96
Tweedmouth 33
'tweel' 133, 158
twinsets 156–7
Twizel and Straw Ford 86
Tyne River 19, 31
Tynedale 4, 87
Tyneside 10
Tyr Haebbe Us, Ye Tyr Ye Odin 62

Uchtred, son of Scot 70
underwear manufacture 127, 136, 139, 142, 147–8, 156, 165
Union armies in American Civil War 139
Unofficial Championship 158, 160, 176
Uplands, Southern 9, 28
Upper Teviotdale 28, 101
Upper Tweed 28
Urbgen 37
Urien, King of Rheged 37

vallum (ditch) 43
Vertish Hill 113
Vespasian, Emperor 30, 31
Vézère River 15
Via Tornabuoni 172
Victoria, Queen of the United Kingdom 128
  Albert and, love of Highlands and all things tartan 133
Vikings, 'Sons of Death' 61
Virgin Mary 74
Votadini 28, 29, 31
Wagga, royal reeve of Carlisle 56
Wales 9
Wales, Prince of 133, 157
Wall Street Crash 161
Walter, the Chaplain 70
Walter de Bolebec 70
Wanderers R.F.C. 177
War Memorial list 152
Wark Castle 85
Wars of Independence 75–81
Waterloo, Battle of 126
Watson, Provost 146
Watson's Spinning Mill 129
Waverley Line 133, 175
Waverley (Scott, W.) 132
Waverley Station 133
Wearyall Hill, Glastonbury 42
Wee Grey Fergies 171
Weisz, Otto 156, 157, 171, 184
Welsh, W.B. 160
Wessex, kings of 62
West Boonraw 47
West Port 52, 115
Westenders 52
Western Front 149, 152
Western Toll 130
Westla 110, 115, 116, 130
White, Rev. Gilbert of Selbourne, Hampshire 44
Whitekirk, East Lothian 57
Whitmuir 112
wick ('farm') 45
William, Duke of Normandy 65
William, nephew of the Earl 70
William II Rufus 66
William the Conqueror 66
Wilson and Glenny 158
Wilton Camp 164

Wilton Cemetery 173
Wilton Flour Mill 129
Wilton Lodge 16
Wilton Lodge Park 16, 33, 35
Windsor Castle 69
winter weather 139, 160
Wintownmoss 83
Wolsey, Cardinal 5, 95
Wood, John 128, 129
Woodnorton 145
Workington Rugby League 142
World War One 148, 149
Yarrow Valley 45, 49, 117
Yeavering 57
Yeavering Bell, near Wooler 38
Yeavering rock 39
Yetholm 121
yew trees in churchyards 44
Y-fronts 161
Y.M. R.F.C. 177
York 31
York, Duke of 127
Young Wolf (Ascelin of Breherval) 65, 67